Guiding Curriculum Decisions for Middle-Grades Language Arts

Margaret Russell Ciardi
Ilene Kantrov
Lynn T. Goldsmith

with assistance from
Anne Shure

Series Editors:
Ilene Kantrov
Lynn T. Goldsmith

HEINEMANN
Portsmouth, NH

Heinemann
A division of Reed Elsevier Inc.
361 Hanover Street
Portsmouth, NH 03801–3912
www.heinemann.com

Offices and agents throughout the world

© 2001 by Education Development Center, Inc.
55 Chapel St., Newton, MA 02458-1060
617-969-7100
www.edc.org

Library of Congress Cataloging-in-Publication Data
ISBN 0-325-00418-8
CIP data is on file with the Library of Congress.

Cover design: Dorothy Geiser

Printed in the United States of America on acid-free paper

05   04   03   02   01   VP   1   2   3   4   5

Contents

Acknowledgments

One of the most rewarding parts of completing a project like this guide is the opportunity to thank the people who have participated in its development. The guide has benefited from the contributions of a substantial number of colleagues, and it is our distinct pleasure to acknowledge them here.

Without the foresight and support of Hayes Mizell, program director at the Edna McConnell Clark Foundation, and Leah Meyer Austin, program director at the W.K. Kellogg Foundation, this guide series would never have come about. Hayes and Leah, along with their colleagues from the National Forum to Accelerate Middle-Grades Reform, have championed the efforts to reanimate middle-grades education nationwide. Through their foundations, Hayes and Leah have been providing support to a number of districts and schools throughout the country to promote standards-based instruction. As they worked with their grantees, they learned that many of these districts have faced considerable challenges in identifying and implementing high-quality curriculum materials. Hayes and Leah recognized that educators were in need of more assistance in making curriculum decisions that will promote academic excellence in their districts, schools, and classrooms.

Nancy Ames, our colleague at Education Development Center, Inc. (EDC), who guides the National Forum and shares its members' commitment to middle-grades reform, had the initial vision for this project. Her work provided a solid and substantial foundation from which to build, and she supported our efforts throughout.

EDC has been a supportive environment for this work. Nancy and other colleagues helped us to shape the focus of this guide series and to frame its content; still others helped us interview teachers, work out conceptual knots, and prepare the manuscript. Our project staff spent many hours thinking and talking through the overall plan for the guide series: thanks to Barbara Brauner Berns, Christine Brown, Michele Browne, Doris Santamaria Makang, Kristin Metz, Nadine Nelson, Marian Pasquale, Anne Shure, and Marianne Thompson. Anne Shure displayed her incomparable interviewing skills and contributed to the writing as well as planning. Shelley Isaacson also did some preliminary research. Mark Driscoll and Barbara Miller displayed their usual collegial generosity in helping us think through a number of difficult questions and issues. Christine Brown helped us stay on track. Deborah Clark picked up loose ends in the final months and supervised the manuscript production with her signature skill and good humor. Other members of the design and production team included Jennifer Davis-Kay, Dorothy Geiser, Gail Hedges, Catherine Lee, Jennifer Roscoe, and Jane Wilson. Thanks to Kristen Bjork for her design consultations.

It was our good fortune to have assembled an encouraging and thoughtful advisory board whose members helped us to plunge into the task with fortitude and enthusiasm. Members included Ron Adams, Loretta Brady, Everly Broadway, Nancy Clark-Chiarelli, Gerard Consuegra, John D'Auria, Georgette Gonsalves, Kristi Kahl, Lloyda King, Greg Kniseley, Gerald Kulm, Joan Lipsitz, Barbara Reys, Linda Rief, Karen Smith, Albert Talborn, Rob Traver, and Anne Wheelock. We would like to extend a special thanks to Nancy Clark-Chiarelli, Kristi Kahl, Joan Lipsitz, Linda Rief, and Anne Wheelock for their careful reviews of portions of the manuscript. Anne in particular made a tremendous contribution to shaping the content of the critical questions and practitioner stories in the science guide, which carried over to this guide as well.

Finally, we would like to extend our thanks to the practitioners who took the time to share their thoughts and experiences with us—their voices can be heard throughout the guide—and to the reviewers who reacted to portions of our manuscripts. These include Geri Belle, Kathleen Bisson, Vera Blake, Sharon Breitenstein, Jennifer Bryant, Stacey Casanave, Bill Chiquelin, Ruth Diane Cichocki, Toby Kahn Curry, Mark Destler, Ree Dillon, Fred Ducat, Ellen Eberly, Leslie Jo Elmore, Pam Fortier, Laura Graham, Brian Haas, Lynette Herring-Harris, Sandra Hollingsworth, Christi Howarth, Lew Kerns, Joellen Killion, Jed Lippert, Brett Mayhan, Ashley McDonald, Shirley Mullin, Julie Nann, Timothy O'Brien, Sara Oelkers, Jeri Ortego, Cecelia Osborn, Nancy Patterson, Melody Raymond, Laura Roop, Leah Robertson, Stephanie Robins, Jane Skelton, Natalie Solomon, Cathy Tabor, Jennifer Tendero, Lillian Villarreal, and Anne Walker. We also thank Kathleen Daniel and Julie Koenig of Holt, Rinehart & Winston for helping us to understand the influence of standards on language arts textbook publishers.

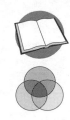

INTRODUCTION

Aiming for Academic Excellence in Middle-Grades Curricula

Third period ends with a few, hurried instructions about homework from the teacher as students pack up their pens, pencils, and notebooks. They pour into the halls, moving in small packs to their next classes. Some scurry and others adopt a leisurely stroll, using the time to catch up with friends. The energy bounces off the lockers lining the corridors. Waves of students surge through open classroom doors—they plop books onto desks and slide into their seats. A soft sigh slips into the emptying hallways as students unpack those pens, pencils, and notebooks and prepare to think and work hard.

When classroom doors close and lessons begin, we want our children to be intellectually challenged and engaged by their work. And indeed, good things are happening in many middle-grades classrooms throughout the country. Students are learning to think deeply about the subjects they are studying and are enthusiastic about their coursework. Their work requires them to think hard, explain and support their ideas, and apply their understanding to new situations.

How can we extend these conditions to more students in more schools? The answer involves making a number of interconnected changes: establishing district policies that promote and support quality instruction, adopting clearly articulated standards for student learning and performance, using high-quality curricula, improving teacher education, providing ongoing professional development for teachers already in the classroom, and developing community support. This guide will help educators address one of these areas of change—designing and using high-quality curriculum to promote high standards of student achievement. *Guiding Curriculum Decisions for Middle-Grades Language Arts* is part of a series of curriculum guides for middle-grades language arts,

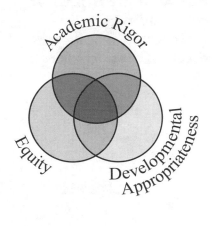

Good things are happening in many middle-grades classrooms throughout the country. Students are learning to think deeply about the subjects they are studying and are enthusiastic about their coursework. Their work requires them to think hard, explain and support their ideas, and apply their understanding to new situations.

In order to meet these standards, teachers face new academic and pedagogical challenges. They must teach more demanding and extensive subject area content, they must develop different instructional strategies, and they must reach a wider range of students. Having a high-quality curriculum to guide instruction is a key to meeting these challenges.

mathematics, science, and social studies.[1] This guide offers a set of principles for making curriculum decisions and illustrates these principles with practitioners' descriptions of their experiences in implementing standards-based curricula.

This guide series was developed at Education Development Center, Inc. with the support of the Edna McConnell Clark and W.K. Kellogg Foundations. It is based on interviews with more than 100 middle-grades educators who are using standards-based curriculum approaches and materials in their districts, schools, and classrooms. This introductory chapter sets the scene for the scope of the guide series, focusing on language arts but drawing examples more broadly from all of the major middle-grades subject areas.

The need for new approaches to curriculum and instruction is clear. Over the past fifteen years educators have been taking a hard look at American students' academic performance. Educators and employers alike express concerns about the educational accomplishments of America's youth. American students are out-performed by peers in many other countries. Within the last decade each major subject area has developed academic standards that raise the bar for student achievement and perform-ance.[2] In order to meet these standards, teachers face new aca-demic and pedagogical challenges. They must teach more demanding and extensive subject area content, they must develop different instructional strategies, and they must reach a wider range of students. Having a high-quality curriculum to guide instruction is a key to meeting these challenges.

While the school or district may specify a grammar text or litera-ture anthology to use, or stipulate particular novels for students to read, most language arts teachers construct their own curriculum

---

[1] The anticipated publication date for the social studies guide is 2002.

[2] In 1989 the National Council of Teachers of Mathematics (NCTM) was the first national organization to produce a set of K-12 curriculum standards for a major subject area. Since then, the National Council of Teachers of English (NCTE) and the International Reading Association (IRA) have collaborated on language arts standards; the National Research Council (NRC) and Project 2061 of the American Association for the Advancement of Science (AAAS) have each pub-lished science standards (the AAAS uses the term "benchmarks" instead of "stan-dards"), and the National Council for the Social Studies (NCSS) has authored social studies standards. In addition, the National Center on Education and the Economy has published *New Standards™ Student Performance Standards* for lan-guage arts, mathematics, science, and applied learning. Information about sub-ject area standards can be found on the websites of all of these organizations.

from these and other components. The availability and use of published curriculum materials are more limited in language arts than in other subject areas. We have puzzled a good deal about why this is the case since, in principle, it should be no more of a challenge to develop and publish quality curriculum materials for language arts than for other subject area disciplines. Although we have no definitive answer to our own question, it does seem that several factors contribute to this situation. Language arts curriculum tends to be less prescriptive in part because the content is less constrained. Language arts teachers have a huge range of choices of literature to teach. Moreover, the skills and processes that students learn in language arts overlap with a variety of other subject areas. Another factor is the desire of teachers to tailor language arts experiences to the particular circumstances of their own students. In addition, perhaps because so much of the content of language arts is literature and writing, realms of creativity and personal expression, language arts teachers tend to guard their autonomy with particular zeal.

What do we mean by "curriculum"?

In a broad sense, curriculum refers to the ideas, skills, processes, and dispositions that educators and content specialists identify as the important ones for students to learn. Many states and districts have developed curriculum frameworks that articulate these learning goals. (Districts may further refine this articulation by indicating the concepts and skills to be learned at each grade level.) The written lessons, activities, exercises, and supporting materials provide the means through which teachers engage students in learning, articulating the important content to teach and offering teachers a structure and organization for instruction. Language arts teachers build their curriculum programs by defining their goals for student learning and planning activities and selecting materials that will support those goals.

Adapted from Lynn T. Goldsmith, June Mark, and Ilene Kantrov, *Choosing a Standards-Based Mathematics Curriculum* (Portsmouth, NH: Heinemann, 2000), 2. Copyright © 1998 by Education Development Center, Inc., K-12 Mathematics Curriculum Center. Published by Heinemann, a division of Reed Elsevier, Inc., Portsmouth, NH.

We have designed *Guiding Curriculum Decisions for Middle-Grades Language Arts* to help language arts educators make their curriculum decisions in thoughtful and principled ways. Like its companion guides for the other major subject areas, this guide includes:

- Critical questions that embody a set of principles to guide curriculum decision making.

- Vignettes about curriculum design and implementation that use practitioners' own voices to illustrate how the principles are addressed in practice.

- Curriculum profiles that provide examples of standards-based language arts curriculum programs.

- An annotated list of other resources that may be useful to curriculum decision making.

The principles we propose to guide decision making are general ones that pertain to any subject area. They articulate three essential components of any academically excellent curriculum—academic rigor, equity, and developmental appropriateness. These three components provide the foundation on which the guides are based. The next section introduces these components, and is followed by some additional information about this guide: a brief tour of the remaining chapters of the guide and a description of our process for identifying and interviewing practitioners about their experiences bringing the standards into their classroom instruction.

Principles to Guide Curriculum Decisions: Three Components of Academically Excellent Curricula

The framework we describe below specifies three key components of academically excellent curricula—academic rigor, equity, and developmental appropriateness. These components were first proposed by members of the National Forum to Accelerate Middle-Grades Reform, a coalition of funders, educators, researchers, state and local leaders, and representatives of national associations that promotes a vision of effective schools for young adolescents.[3] The three components are illustrated by the diagram of interlocking circles pictured throughout this introduction. This section describes each of the components and discusses how each pertains to middle-grades students.

---

[3] Joan Lipsitz, Hayes Mizell, Anthony Jackson, and Leah Meyer Austin, "Speaking With One Voice," *Phi Delta Kappan*, 78, no. 7 (1997): 553.

A view of middle-grades students

"Teaching middle school is like being inside a kaleidoscope—the view of the kids is always changing, and it's always interesting. I've heard middle-grades kids described in a lot of ways—mostly contradictory. For example, they're really learning how to take responsibility for themselves; they're really wild. They're vigilantly watching everyone and everything around them so they can figure out who they are; they're completely oblivious to the rest of the world. They're kind and thoughtful; they're rude and obnoxious. You can get someone in this school to agree to every one of these descriptions, and most of us would say that, at one time or another, they're *all* true.

"I think about middle-grades students like kernels of popcorn. They pretty much all enter sixth grade as young kids, and during the three years we have them, they start popping at different rates, transforming into these new adolescent creatures. The most obvious part of the transformation is the physical one. There are always a few kids who enter the sixth grade looking 16 instead of 11 or 12 (or who are older to begin with because they've repeated grades somewhere along the way), but mostly the sixth graders still have the bodies of children. And then, they start popping. By the end of the first year, there are a handful of boys who are shooting up and have feet the size of canal boats, and a bunch of girls who are beginning to look like young women. When everyone comes back to school the next fall, there are more kids who are making the change, and during seventh grade, even more. It's fun to watch friends catch up with each other—one month, two boys will walk down the hall looking like Mutt and Jeff, and two or three months later, they're standing shoulder to shoulder. By the time they leave for the high school, better than half of the girls are taller than I am—and let's not even talk about the boys!

"These kids are such a funny mix of becoming more grown up emotionally and intellectually and still remaining quite young. I really enjoy their class discussions, because you can see the kids revving up their mental engines. They're thinking deeply and figuring out some really sophisticated stuff. Kids will argue for their ideas and make pretty convincing cases, too. Even though they're beginning to become really passionate about some of their ideas and beliefs, they're also learning to listen to other people. Lots of times they can understand why someone else might see things differently. Sometimes they can even convince others to change their minds.

"But this growing intellectual power is only part of the story. Kids can be having this really intense and interesting discussion in class, say about how to control variables in an experimental design. Then, as soon as class ends, the girls may shift seamlessly into a debate about the 'hottest' TV star on their way out the door and the boys may start to talk up the latest basketball game or exchange tips for avoiding skateboard wipe-outs."

— Middle-grades educator

Academic rigor: Meeting high standards

The current efforts to set standards for student performance at national, state, and district levels are, in essence, efforts to define academic rigor. At the heart of the standards movement is the question, "What is the essential knowledge of the discipline?" Or, as one Massachusetts teacher has put it, the fundamental question is, "What do I want my students to know ten years after they've been in my class?" For reform-minded educators the answer to these questions includes understanding the major concepts of a subject area (the "big ideas"), acquiring characteristic ways of thinking within the discipline ("habits of mind"), and learning its particular methods of investigation and argumentation. The answer also includes mastering skills, facts, and useful procedures, but it reframes these as part of a larger intellectual enterprise rather than as the primary goal of curriculum and instruction.

Standards are more than a list of expectations for student accomplishment—they're not simply a scope and sequence for the topics to be covered over the course of a year, a grade level, or an entire K–12 career. Standards are guideposts to help keep students on track for learning the fundamental ideas of the subject area, reasoning according to the methods and conventions of the discipline, and presenting (and, if necessary, defending) their thinking to others.

This view of standards is pushing curriculum and instruction in new directions. Drawing on models of apprenticeship-style learning and on the theory that students construct their knowledge and understanding by actively engaging with the central ideas of a discipline, the current educational reform movement focuses on creating opportunities for students to build and use their understanding in rich and complex learning contexts.

An academically rigorous curriculum articulates a clear set of goals for learning. It gives teachers and students a reasonable picture of the nature of the discipline and connects them with the same kinds of work that engage professional practitioners. For example, students research and write persuasive essays, make and test mathematical conjectures, or design science experiments to test hypotheses. A rigorous curriculum helps students exercise general reasoning processes, develop ways of thinking that are particular to the subject area, and acquire an understanding of the methods for establishing and evaluating knowledge in the discipline. For example, the language arts curriculum should help students read and write about complex ideas, think critically, and understand the criteria by which we judge a well-reasoned essay, while mathematics classes should help students develop an appreciation for the characteristics of a convincing mathematical argument.

In addition, a rigorous curriculum offers students (and teachers) a coherent view of the subject area by making connections among important ideas within the discipline. These connections have an effect similar to that of viewing an Impressionist painting from across a room. From up close, the painting looks like little more than individual patches of color floating on the surface of the canvas. From a distance, these colors coalesce into the rendering of a three-dimensional scene. A rigorous curriculum offers connections that help students recognize and appreciate the recurring themes, ideas, and methodologies of the discipline instead of only small, isolated pieces of the picture. In addition, it emphasizes connections between classroom study and real-world applications, helping students to recognize the practical utility of their developing knowledge. Finally, a rigorous curriculum uses a variety of strategies for assessing students' understanding and ability to apply their knowledge to new problems or in different contexts.

In the particular case of the middle grades, it is important that curricula not underestimate students' intellectual capabilities. Early adolescence is a time of significant growth in reasoning capacity, and students' coursework should reflect their increasing ability to think hypothetically and systematically. Jean Piaget, the grand master of cognitive developmental psychology, characterized the young adolescent as navigating the final major stage of intellectual growth.[4] Young adolescents become increasingly adept at considering a variety of perspectives, examining situations from different angles, assessing contingencies, and acknowledging

---

[4] For an introduction to Piaget's theories, see Herbert Ginsburg and Sylvia Opper, Piaget's *Theory of Intellectual Development* (Englewood Cliffs, NJ: Prentice-Hall, 1969), or Jean Piaget, "Piaget's Theory," in *Carmichael's Handbook of Child Development*, ed. P. H. Mussen (New York: Wiley, 1970), 702–732.

Standards are guideposts to help keep students on track for learning the fundamental ideas of the subject area, reasoning according to the methods and conventions of the discipline, and presenting (and, if necessary, defending) their thinking to others.

An academically rigorous curriculum for the middle grades acknowledges students' growing cognitive capacities and provides them with intellectual challenges to help them shape and sharpen their growing interests.

possible outcomes. They can think about what might happen (or what might have happened if conditions had been different). Their reasoning becomes more complex and systematic as they develop the capacity to coordinate their thinking about several ideas at once. A classic example is the young adolescent's developing ability to understand that a balance beam's balance point is affected by the coordination of several factors: the amount of weight on each arm, the placement of the weights, and the location of the fulcrum.

The typical middle-grades curriculum is often criticized as a rehash of previous material, a time for review to ensure that students are prepared for their work in high school. Students are often seen as marking time instead of encountering new ideas and challenging work. An academically rigorous curriculum for the middle grades acknowledges students' growing cognitive capacities and provides them with intellectual challenges to help them shape and sharpen their growing interests. It helps students develop their reasoning abilities and their capabilities for inquiry. It also helps them learn to monitor and critique their work by tapping their growing "metacognitive" ability—the capacity to guide their learning by reflecting critically on their own thinking.

Many schools have looked to using interdisciplinary approaches as a way to create more overall curricular coherence and enriching experiences for students. The team structures common in many middle schools can facilitate this effort by providing opportunities for teachers to work more closely together to establish and coordinate lesson plans. In some schools, the same teacher may be responsible for instruction in more than one subject area. In addition to emphasizing connections among different disciplines, interdisciplinary studies have the potential to explore subject area content in much richer and more realistic contexts. After all, the activities and studies that comprise adult work rarely require the skills and ideas of only a single discipline.

It is important, however, to beware of a potential pitfall to interdisciplinary studies. In practice, it is less common to create a truly interdisciplinary curriculum than it is to integrate some of the themes, skills, and tools of one discipline into the study of another. For example, it is becoming increasingly common to ask students in mathematics class to write about their solution strategies, or even to write and present reports. This is a valuable addition to mathematics classes, as it provides opportunities for students to articulate their thinking and use communication skills. However, teachers rarely respond to this written work as they would to writing assignments in language arts class. It would be unusual for teachers to require several drafts of writing done in mathematics class in order to help students to clarify their ideas, shape their reasoning, and produce effective and grammatically correct prose. Writing assignments may integrate language arts skills into mathematics class, but they generally are not treated with equal weight. Similarly, having students read a novel about the Revolutionary War in language arts class while they study the colonial period in social studies does not, in itself, constitute an interdisciplinary approach to language arts and social studies. But a truly interdisciplinary curriculum addresses the full set of academic standards for each subject area involved, and requires more time than is allotted for study of a single subject.

Equity: Holding *all* students to high standards

Our public education system is built on the commitment to prepare all of the country's children for productive lives as adult members of our society. Unfortunately, the realization of this commitment has been imperfect, and it is often those students at most risk for being marginalized—those with the fewest resources and poorest prospects—who receive the least adequate education.[5] By articulating high standards for all students, the current education reform movement raises expectations for student performance, with particular attention to students who have traditionally not excelled in school. Hand in hand with these higher expectations comes the assumption that all students can learn important concepts and skills when instruction builds from their current understanding, focuses on making learning meaningful, and engages students' intellectual strengths to drive the learning process.

Educators who embrace this assumption commit themselves to finding a wide range of instructional approaches and classroom activities in order to meet the specific learning needs of individual students. In the past, the most common approach for working

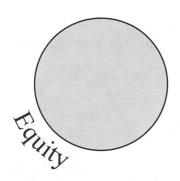

Equity

Hand in hand with these higher expectations comes the assumption that all students can learn important concepts and skills when instruction builds from their current understanding, focuses on making learning meaningful, and engages students' intellectual strengths to drive the learning process.

---

[5] Some also make the case that our educational system fails to meet the needs of very academically oriented students, who would benefit from more accelerated and in-depth learning.

An equitable curriculum promotes high levels of achievement among a wide range of students by having more than one way to convey ideas and help students acquire skills.

with students at risk of falling behind has been to "re-teach," going over material students have previously failed to learn by using similar (if not identical) explanations and exercises in the hopes that more exposure will eventually lead to greater understanding. This "more of the same" approach is the educational equivalent of trying to communicate with someone who doesn't speak a word of English by repeating yourself, taking extra care to enunciate clearly and to speak more slowly and more loudly. If the listener has no way to make sense of your speech in the first place, you won't accomplish much by saying it again. You might, however, make some progress if you try something different, like supplementary gestures or even pantomime.

An equitable curriculum promotes high levels of achievement among a wide range of students by having more than one way to convey ideas and help students acquire skills. It includes approaches and activities that accommodate a variety of learning styles and provides different kinds of opportunities for students to gain understanding of the subject area content and demonstrate their knowledge and skill. For example, in language arts classes, students might read aloud as well as silently; create story webs to help them follow the plot and structure of their reading selections; view video versions of the literature they are using in class; act out parts of the stories themselves; and express their ideas in essays, journal responses, artistic renderings, and oral presentations. By offering a variety of approaches, equitable curricula make it possible for students with different cognitive strengths and preferred ways of accessing information to grapple with the important ideas of the curriculum. However, because students have different "ways in" to the material does not mean that they can stop working to strengthen areas of weakness. When a teacher shows a video of *The Island of the Blue Dolphins* in class, she may make it possible for a struggling reader to follow the plot of the story and engage in discussions about themes of loss and self-reliance. But showing the video is not a substitute for helping the student become a more fluent and competent reader. This work still remains to be done.

An equitable curriculum offers content that is rich and deep enough that students with different levels of understanding can all extend their learning. Both the kinds of topics addressed and the kinds of work students are asked to do must be sufficiently broad to allow everyone room to learn. In language arts, learning activities can offer all students the chance to analyze literature, discuss and defend their perspectives, and practice writing in different genres. An equitable curriculum creates opportunities for all students, not just the most successful, to do work that challenges them to take charge of their work, reason, organize their thoughts, and communicate them to others. As educator and author Anne Wheelock has observed, "All students can benefit from the thinking skills and enrichment activities often offered only to those labeled 'gifted' and 'talented.'"[6]

Student diversity takes a number of forms: different approaches to learning; gender-related differences; a variety of home cultures, languages, and life experiences; different forms of physical challenge. Curricula should be sensitive to such differences. The contexts (and, where appropriate, content) should represent a variety of perspectives and experiences. The work and lives of those "dead, white, European males" are only part of the picture. An equitable curriculum broadens the traditional canon, ensuring that all parts of the picture are developed.

How do issues of equity apply to middle-grades curricula in particular? Curricula for young adolescents need to be particularly sensitive to providing all students with opportunities to exercise their newly developing logical and critical thinking skills. Because early adolescence is a time of intellectual growth spurts as well as physical ones, middle-grades students are developing their new cognitive resources and capacities at different rates and times. A typical middle-grades classroom, therefore, is likely to contain students with an especially wide range of cognitive resources and capabilities. This intensifies the challenge of creating curricula that can promote learning for students who bring a range of skills, prior knowledge, and reasoning abilities into the classroom.

Developmental appropriateness: Attending to characteristics of young adolescents

Effective curricula are geared to the students they are designed to reach. Their subject area content is developed at a level of complexity that builds on students' current knowledge and encourages them to push toward deeper and more extensive understanding.

---

[6] Anne Wheelock, *Crossing the Tracks* (New York: The New Press, 1992), 13.

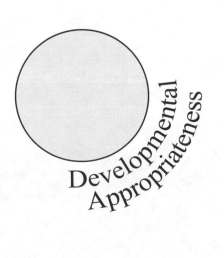

Developmental Appropriateness

An equitable curriculum creates opportunities for all students, not just the most successful, to do work that challenges them to take charge of their work, reason, organize their thoughts, and communicate them to others.

In the middle grades, a developmentally appropriate curriculum takes into account the young adolescent's growing cognitive capacities.

If the ideas developed in the curriculum are too far removed from students' experience or current ways of understanding, they will be too difficult to grasp; if the ideas are too simplistic, students will be bored by work they already understand. Developmentally appropriate curricula are based on knowledge of how students' thinking develops. This ensures that the curricula deal with central ideas and skills in ways that address students' typical questions, confusions, and evolving understandings. As they develop curriculum, language arts educators use their own experiences with students, along with educational and psychological research regarding children's acquisition of subject area concepts and skills, to address the needs of all their middle-grades students.

Curricula must not only engage students at an appropriate intellectual level; they must engage students' interest and attention as well. Unless students are motivated to connect to the ideas in the curriculum, they will just mark time with studies that they don't "own." Developmentally appropriate curricula must therefore set students' academic work in contexts that are suited to their age and interests.

In the middle grades, a developmentally appropriate curriculum takes into account the young adolescent's growing cognitive capacities, helping students move from their informal and intuitive ways of understanding toward more formal and systematic approaches to the subjects they are studying. It is also particularly important that curricula motivate and engage middle-grades students, since young adolescents begin to question the purpose and value of adult-initiated assignments. As many students move to the middle grades, they leave their tractability behind as a souvenir for their elementary school teachers. Many students become less willing to work hard simply because a teacher requests it, asking, "What's the use of learning about this?" Students are more likely to put effort into their schoolwork when they perceive the contexts for lessons and activities to be interesting, important, and relevant to their lives. A developmentally appropriate middle-grades curriculum capitalizes on students' growing interest in their own communities, other cultures, and other eras to motivate their studies.

On the social front, the young adolescent's more flexible and far-reaching ways of thinking lead to a seeming paradox: an increasing attention to others which is paired with a growing self-consciousness.

Students in the middle grades begin to think more deeply about the consequences of people's thoughts and actions, and are willing to consider complex and important questions like, "What makes a good friend?" "What does it mean to be a slave, or a slaveholder?" "What do the statistics on driving age and accident rates tell us?" "What is the effect of human activity on the environment?" Middle-grades students also think a lot about their own role in the world. Their questions about identity aren't idle ones. With bodies that often look and feel alien, and with newly emerging observational and analytic skills, young adolescents are often genuinely in a state of flux. As middle-grades students grapple with questions about themselves and their world, they turn to their compatriots in struggle—their peers—for self-definition and validation.

Developmentally appropriate curricula for the middle grades capitalize on this attention to self and peers by offering students opportunities to develop social skills and to use their classmates as resources for learning. Because middle-grades students are particularly oriented toward their peer group, providing them opportunities to work together offers a way to harness their keen interest in one another toward productive educational ends. Students can develop their collaborative skills as well as engage their capacity to compare and critique ideas from different perspectives.

A caution. A common misinterpretation of standards-based reform is that it is first and foremost about offering students motivating and engaging activities. But an effort directed only at making lessons appealing and engaging may lead to trivial intellectual work—in an effort to hook students on learning, students may be let off the hook of mastering content.

Choosing fun classroom activities, using concrete, "hands-on" lessons, and having students work in cooperative groups do not by themselves guarantee student learning. Without clear academic goals and an understanding of how to reach them, efforts to provide engaging and interesting activities are simply form without substance. Although subject area standards all stress the importance of student involvement, educators should not assume that active and engaged students provide adequate evidence that substantial learning is taking place.

There is no question that it is better for students to find their work engaging and interesting than to be bored and unconvinced of the value of their efforts. However, activities may prove engaging

Developmentally appropriate curricula for the middle grades capitalize on this attention to self and peers by offering students opportunities to develop social skills and to use their classmates as resources for learning.

without stretching students' understanding. When this is the case, neither the criterion for academic rigor nor that for developmental appropriateness is being met. Quality education isn't simply about having students busy and happy in the classroom. It's about having them engaged in work that has intellectual teeth.

Integrating the three components

Only when all three components described above are present can a curriculum offer the intellectual depth and pedagogical perspectives that create powerful learning opportunities for a wide range of students. Academic excellence lies at the intersection of academic rigor, equity, and developmental appropriateness.

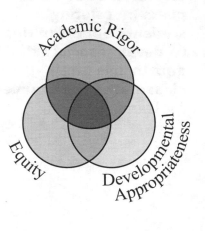

Because the three components work in concert to support learning, when one or another is missing or weak, the curriculum will not promote academic excellence. Without academic rigor, the curriculum will have no edge as a tool for intellectual growth and students will be denied important resources for building knowledge and understanding. However, if an academically rigorous curriculum is inequitable (by being successful at promoting learning for only a narrow segment of the student population), its effectiveness is also compromised. It runs the risk of shortchanging students who have interesting minds and the potential to make significant contributions, but whose modes of learning or whose academic or social experiences are inconsistent with the limited approaches taken by the curriculum. And even an admirably rigorous curriculum will fail to promote learning if it does not address students' typical patterns of developing concepts and skills, or if it fails to capture students' interest or attention. In curriculum, as in other aspects of life, a balance among important components is the key.

About This Guide

This guide, like the others in the series, uses the framework described above to examine standards-based curricula and their implementation. It also relies on the insights of a number of teachers and advisors, who shared with us their thoughts and observations about using standards-based approaches to curriculum. In addition to providing information about the implementation of particular curriculum approaches, they talked about the "big picture"—how curriculum related to their standards for student performance, the instructional approaches they saw as most effective for student learning in diverse populations, and their commitment to professional development. Below is a summary of the contents of *Guiding Curriculum Decisions for Middle-Grades Language Arts.*

A brief tour of the guide

Guiding Curriculum Decisions for Middle-Grades Language Arts looks at curriculum from several different perspectives. The introduction has offered a set of principles—the three components of academically excellent curricula—as an overarching guide to curriculum decision making. Subsequent chapters use these principles as a framework for considering curriculum decision making and implementation.

Chapter 1. In this chapter, we look at practitioners' experiences to help us draw explicit connections between these principles and the ways teachers actually plan and implement curricula to promote students' learning. We want this guide to speak to educators (teachers, curriculum specialists, staff developers, principals, and central office administrators) from the place where, ultimately, the work of the curriculum is carried out—the classroom. By grounding the guide in practitioners' own descriptions of their experiences, we aim to give readers a fuller and more vibrant picture of what makes an excellent curriculum excellent.

The chapter is organized around "critical questions" to ask when making curriculum decisions. These questions are tied to the three critical components of academically excellent curricula we have described above: academic rigor, equity, and developmental appropriateness. Each of the critical questions is then illustrated by vignettes with practitioners' observations of ways they (or their districts) have addressed the question.

Chapter 2. This chapter offers two profiles that are examples of standards-based language arts curriculum. The first profile was developed by a group of sixth-grade teachers. We developed the second. These profiles are intended as models for how to go about constructing a comprehensive, year-by-year curriculum that uses high-quality literature and that addresses national standards for reading, writing, speaking, and listening. These profiles are also designed to give you a sense of the complexity of the curriculum development process.

> **We want this guide to speak to educators . . . from the place where, ultimately, the work of the curriculum is carried out—the classroom.**

Chapter 3. This final chapter provides an annotated list of additional resources to assist you in making curriculum decisions. These resources include standards and frameworks, professional organizations, websites, curricula that provide teachers with professional development opportunities, professional development resources, published literature programs and anthologies, management tools, and examples of books that provide both theoretical and practical guidance about language arts curriculum, teaching, and learning.

Interviews with language arts educators

In preparing this guide, we spoke to a number of language arts educators throughout the country about their language arts curricula. We were interested in learning from them about district- and classroom-level curriculum choices and decisions, their thoughts about different curriculum materials and approaches, some of the challenges they had encountered in implementing standards-based curricula, and ways they had resolved those challenges.

The 40 language arts educators we interviewed for this guide included a curriculum coordinator from a large urban district in California, a staff developer for a group of districts in the Midwest, a teacher in New York City, and another working on a reservation in the Southwest. We identified educators to interview in several ways. Colleagues and members of the advisory board for this guide recommended practitioners they knew and respected. Sometimes these practitioners, in turn, recommended that we speak with colleagues of theirs. Curriculum developers also recommended teachers who were familiar with standards-based instruction and articulate about meeting the challenges of implementing a standards-based curriculum. We also contacted several of the curriculum supervisors and coordinators whose districts were associated with our granting agencies, the Edna McConnell Clark and W.K. Kellogg Foundations. The practitioners in this last group were quite helpful in assisting us to develop a fuller picture of the kinds of challenges that teachers face as they work to meet standards in their classrooms.

The interviews themselves consisted of conversations of approximately an hour in length, which followed a flexible interview protocol. The interviews included descriptions of standards-based language arts curricula teachers had developed, discussion of the literature and other resources teachers included in these curricula, ways that local and state standards influenced teachers' curricular decisions, and approaches to working with students who were succeeding or struggling in class. We have used these interviews in creating the vignettes in Chapter 1 and in developing the example grades 6–8 curriculum profiled in Chapter 2.

A final word

As we have worked on this guide, we have spoken with many teachers who have come to believe that a standards-based curriculum has helped them to teach better because it has helped them focus on providing rigorous, equitable, and developmentally appropriate instruction for their students. For many, learning to implement these curricula effectively has been a challenge, but ultimately a rewarding one. We hope that you, too, will find that organizing your curriculum decisions around careful consideration of standards for language arts learning can be a powerful force in your district, school, or classroom. And we hope that this guide will help you to make thoughtful decisions about planning and implementing language arts curriculum in the future.

CHAPTER 1

Critical Questions in Curriculum Decision Making

The three key components of academically excellent curricula described in the introduction provide a framework for educators faced with making curriculum decisions. However, it is one thing to talk in the abstract about the important components of an academically excellent curriculum and another to have an image of what such a creature looks like and how teachers make it work in the classroom with 150 students each day. This chapter focuses on what curricula that are academically rigorous, equitable, and developmentally appropriate look like in action. Drawing on interviews with teachers and school leaders around the U.S. who have experience planning and implementing exemplary language arts curricula, this chapter takes you inside classrooms and schools to see how educators design and use these curricula to promote student learning.

Critical Questions

This chapter poses a set of six "critical questions" to ask about middle-grades curriculum. A series of vignettes—stories told in the voices of practitioners—illustrate how the answers to each question emerge from the intersection of excellent curriculum, effective teaching, and support of school and district leadership.

Five of the six critical questions, and the corresponding sections of this chapter, focus on the components of the curricula themselves—academic rigor, equity, and developmental appropriateness. (Rigor accounts for three of the questions, one focusing on how the curriculum achieves coherence, one on how it supports standards for teaching and learning, and the third on how it integrates literature.) A brief introduction to each section explains the particular aspect of curricular excellence that the question highlights.

> **It is one thing to talk in the abstract about the important components of an academically excellent curriculum and another to have an image of what such a creature looks like and how teachers make it work in the classroom with 150 students each day.**

The last question focuses on the kinds of professional development teachers need in order to effectively plan and implement excellent curricula. The introduction to this section describes why professional development is so important for teachers striving for a standards-based curriculum, and characterizes strategies for effective professional development.

Vignettes

The critical questions are illustrated by one or more vignettes that focus on the curriculum component or implementation issue addressed. Because the qualities of excellent curricula are intertwined, there is some overlap between the vignettes within each section and across different sections. For example, an exemplary curriculum that is academically rigorous will necessarily take advantage of students' growing cognitive capacities in the middle-grades years—a key aspect of developmental appropriateness.

Vignettes also vary in length, usually depending on the complexity of the curriculum features or aspects of professional development that they illustrate.

The names and locations of the teachers, school leaders, and districts in the vignettes are fictional. However, the kinds of districts (for example, urban, rural, suburban, small, large, relatively resource-rich or -poor) and the areas of the country mentioned do correspond to the types of districts and geographical areas represented by the practitioners interviewed. The practitioners' words have also been edited, and in some cases a particular vignette represents a composite of several people's experiences and perspectives. However, the vignettes do reflect the views represented in the interviews on which they were based.

Teachers who design and implement standards-based curricula use a variety of published materials—some as classroom resources and others to guide their planning and instruction. For the most part, the vignettes do not mention particular resources by name, although they do refer to categories of materials such as literature anthologies, and to particular examples of literature selections. The literature selections mentioned are typical of those used by a number of the teachers interviewed, but by no means represent a comprehensive selection of high-quality middle-grades literature. The final section of vignettes, on professional development, focuses on, and names, an example of a published curriculum program that offers professional development support. This is one of several such programs that are described briefly in Chapter 4, along with other examples of the kinds of resources teachers can draw on in planning and implementing standards-based curricula. Teachers in several of the vignettes refer to the authors of some of these resources; a list of references at the end of this chapter identifies examples of these authors' works.

A strong language arts curriculum is coherent, with all the parts connected. It has a deliberate design that focuses on promoting the skills and knowledge students need to achieve high standards. A coherent curriculum:

- Integrates language arts concepts, processes, and skills.

- Builds students' understanding of concepts and mastery of skills and processes over time.

- Makes connections among the different language arts—reading, writing, speaking, and listening.

- Links language arts learning to the real world and allows students to explore ideas that help them make sense of human experience.

- Uses assessments both to inform classroom instruction and to evaluate student achievement.

- Provides scoring guides to students that make clear what they need to know and be able to do.

In addition, because young adolescents are "in the middle"—ready to be challenged intellectually, but still developing the knowledge and skills necessary for more complex work—a coherent middle-grades curriculum must do one more thing. It must build on what students have learned in the elementary grades and set the stage for learning language arts in the high school grades.

There are wide variations in the ways that teachers, schools, and districts interpret these aspects of coherence for curriculum development. The two vignettes that follow illustrate different ways to address the challenge of creating a coherent, standards-based curriculum. One approach involves developing an entirely new curriculum, while the other approach uses language arts standards to guide the modification of an existing curriculum. What both approaches have in common is their focus on

ACADEMIC RIGOR

How can we create a coherent language arts curriculum that has a deliberate and integrated design?

"Basically, the vision our school has is of the student as worker, the teacher as coach, and a lot of hands-on, inquiry-based learning. The various subject areas are organized by domain. Language arts is part of the domain of Arts and Humanities. In this domain, the kids need to demonstrate mastery of six skill areas at the end of eighth grade in order to move on to high school level courses."

important ideas or themes as conceptual organizers for the curriculum. Both approaches also carefully integrate reading, writing, and oral language, and balance attention to concepts, processes, and skills. Both carefully develop students' knowledge and understanding over time. Both also use assessments of student performance to guide teachers in choosing instructional strategies.

Integrating language arts processes and skills around an interdisciplinary theme

Jerry Miller teaches seventh and eighth graders at the Thorndike School, a public charter school in the Northeast. Jerry describes the communities from which students are drawn as "suburban to rural." Thorndike is structured around the principles of the Coalition of Essential Schools, a school reform organization based on the philosophy of educator Theodore Sizer. Jerry explains that "basically, the vision our school has is of the student as worker, the teacher as coach, and a lot of hands-on, inquiry-based learning. The various subject areas are organized by domain. Language arts is part of the domain of Arts and Humanities. In this domain, the kids need to demonstrate mastery of six skill areas at the end of eighth grade in order to move on to high school level courses. So our standards are based on what we expect an eighth grader to master. The six skills in our domain are reading, writing, oral presentation, artistic expression, listening, and research."

The faculty at Thorndike meet to plan the next year's curriculum in July, when students are on vacation. The curriculum is designed to be academically rigorous and challenging, and to bring students up to, and even beyond, the state standards. Jerry explains the curriculum planning process: "Each year our entire curriculum is framed by a central question which is used across all disciplines, so it's a question for the whole school. Then different domains or disciplines approach the question from different angles. We go into our summer planning with only an essential question, and it's the faculty's time to create curriculum. The first week and a half we are usually in brainstorming mode. For example, we are a fairly new school, so the first year the essential question was, 'What is community?' In the second year the question was, 'What is change?'"

Jerry describes how teachers at Thorndike create curriculum around their essential question. "During the first year of the school, we chose an essential question about community because we wanted to establish a sense of community from the get-go. In the spring of that year, we developed a unit that explored how communities respond to differences among the people within them. Our focus, as a school, was the Civil Rights Movement. We read *To Kill A Mockingbird*, while at the same time we were looking at the Thirteenth, Fourteenth, and Fifteenth Amendments, along with the history of the Civil Rights Movement in this country. In visual arts, we studied a series of paintings by Jacob Lawrence called the *Migration* series to learn about the movement of African Americans from the South into urban centers in the North. All of these strands of curriculum were happening simultaneously, so the history was in the service of the language arts, which was also in the service of the visual arts.

"From there, the kids then chose a community that they felt had to face challenges to its unity at some point in the history of this country. Then they chose literature and primary sources that were relevant to their topic. The culminating activity required that students create their own series of paintings that captured the story of their community's response to the challenge. That's an example of how we try to make connections."

Jerry continues, "We also have to weave in various skills and processes that students need in order to communicate. Writing is the one that gets the most emphasis. We incorporate expository, persuasive, and analytic writing. For example, the students read the play *Fences* by August Wilson. Then they had to choose a particular piece of dialogue or a particular interaction between two characters that they found to be insightful or provocative. The corresponding writing assignment was an analytic piece on the significance of that passage. There's also a lot of informal writing, which we do in the form of reader response journals. Students write how they feel and think about what they're reading in these journals. In the earlier grades we give them prompts to respond to on a nightly basis. Then, as they get older, we give them more autonomy with how they use their journals."

Jerry also describes how oral language is woven into the curriculum. "Oral presentation is a very big part of our curriculum. That first year, when we were looking at Martin Luther King as a leader in the Civil Rights Movement, students closely analyzed the 'I Have a Dream' speech. We looked at that speech and identified what aspects of it made an effective piece of oral presentation.

"I was intrigued with [James] Beane's ideas about building a curriculum around a central theme. As I began to think about my curriculum, I chose an overall theme for the year—tolerance. Then I picked critical issues about tolerance for my students to investigate. . . . The theme was like the glue that joined everything together and made each of the parts of the curriculum make sense."

Then students took those qualities and tried to apply them to writing and presenting their own 'Dream' speeches."

All the arts and humanities teachers at Thorndike use rubrics (scoring guides) based on criteria for excellence for each of the six skill areas. Jerry says, "From day one that the students are in the school they become familiar with these criteria for all of the skill areas. We assess on a continuum from 'just beginning,' to 'approaches the standards,' to 'meets or exceeds the standards.' Every time a student does a piece of work he or she is assessed on that continuum for the skill, based on the criteria for excellence."

Jerry notes that the first group of eighth graders in his school did well on the statewide language arts test. But he and the other teachers keep monitoring their curriculum to ensure that it has the appropriate balance of intellectual content and development of language arts processes and skills so that students will continue to achieve high standards.

Moving toward a coherent curriculum that is guided by standards

Susan Barron teaches language arts to 175 eighth graders in an urban middle school in California. While the majority of Susan's students speak English, they represent diverse ethnic groups and home cultures. Teachers at Susan's school are committed to preparing all the students in the school for college or university. Susan notes, "We expect that all students are going to be successful. So our push in middle school is to get them prepared for high school so that all students will go to college."

Susan, who has been teaching eighth grade for 14 years, describes how her curriculum has evolved as she has worked to "keep up" with important trends in the field. A number of years ago she read an article about thematic teaching by middle-grades educator James Beane. "I was intrigued with Beane's ideas about building a curriculum around a central theme. As I began to think about my curriculum, I chose an overall theme for the year—tolerance. Then I picked critical issues about tolerance for my students to investigate. I wanted them to think about tolerance as it relates to culture, language, and gender. I wanted them to think about tolerance and issues of physical appearance. That's important for middle-grades students—they're so concerned with how they look and how other kids look. We thought a lot about tolerance throughout the year. I chose novels and short stories,

Chapter 1/Critical Questions in Curriculum Decision Making planned reading and writing workshops, projects, and field trips—all kinds of opportunities for my students to examine tolerance. The theme was like the glue that joined everything together and made each of the parts of the curriculum make sense."

Susan talks about how the standards recently adopted by her school district have influenced her to further rethink her curriculum. "Before the big push on standards in our district, I had to make all the decisions about what I was going to teach. Now I have to make certain that I teach everything in the district's curriculum guide. I also have to be certain that what I am doing fits with the standards. It's comforting to know exactly what my students should know and be able to do by the end of the year—the kinds of writing and speaking, the skills, the strategies they have to learn, even though this means that I've had to make some changes in my curriculum. At first, it really bothered me. But I'm learning how to make all the pieces fit together without losing the big ideas that I want kids to study. In fact, I think my curriculum is stronger that it was before."

For example, Susan says, "I've always done a unit on the Holocaust as part of my tolerance theme. We read *The Diary of Anne Frank* and the kids did oral presentations about the characters, theme, and plot. That was fine, but now, because of the standards, we do more. When we study the Holocaust, we still read *Anne Frank,* but we also read *Night* by Elie Wiesel and nonfiction selections about the Holocaust. We learn literary elements and strategies for reading fiction *and* nonfiction. We study different text structures—compare and contrast, cause and effect. Then we learn how to write essays that use those structures.

"I've also added a research paper. It's required by the standards. Students pick a topic of their choice related in some way to the theme of tolerance or intolerance. They can study whatever subject they choose. Some of them have done research on the Armenian genocide or the effects of westward expansion on Native Americans. Others have studied the causes and effects of teenage gangs. It depends on their interests. They learn the entire research process. I teach it step by step. Right at the beginning, I give them a rubric [scoring guide] that spells out exactly how their work will be evaluated. I keep going back to the rubric, checking their work against the rubric. What have they learned to do? Which steps of the research process are problematic?

Doing a research paper is challenging and it fits well with the content standards. They've done some really creative work for their presentations, but the content is firmly based in their research. Also, I'm more explicit than I used to be about teaching oral presenting skills. I guess you might say that I teach smarter. I integrate the pieces and they fit together well."

ACADEMIC RIGOR

How will the middle-grades language arts curriculum enable students to meet standards?

Language arts standards at the national, state, and local levels vary widely in terms of their level of detail and degree of prescriptiveness. Some standards describe precisely what students should know and be able to do, and include samples of the kinds of work they might do to demonstrate their learning. Some standards identify the genres of literature students should read, and the historical eras and cultures that literature selections should represent. Some even specify the works of literature that should be read at each grade level. Some standards identify specific literary features and devices students should understand, and the particular grammar, spelling, and other language skills that students should master. Other standards simply lay out broad goals for student learning, such as reading a range of genres and being able to write for different audiences and purposes. For standards to be effective, they have to be specific enough to provide focus and guidance.

Well-conceived standards address, with some specificity:

- Reading to comprehend meaning and interpret text.
- Writing to communicate effectively for different purposes, audiences, and contexts.
- Speaking and listening to gather and share information, persuade others, understand and express ideas, and analyze messages.
- Mastering the skills necessary for effective reading, writing, and oral communication.
- Reading, analyzing, interpreting, and evaluating different kinds of literature, representing a variety of genres, historical periods, and cultures.

Because of the variability in the standards, the specific demands on teachers for interpreting and meeting standards differ depending on what has been adopted by their states and districts. However, in any case, focusing on standards will yield benefits as well as challenges. The benefits of well-conceived and implemented standards include:

- Clearly articulating what all students should learn.
- Setting out challenging norms and high expectations for all students.
- Drawing attention and additional resources to schools with unacceptably low outcomes on standards-based assessments.
- Making school systems and administrators, as well as teachers, accountable for student performance.

The challenges of teaching to standards are closely related to the potential benefits. When the primary focus is on what students must learn instead of on what they should be taught, teachers must organize curricula and instruction around their understanding of students' academic needs. If all students are held to the same high expectations, then those at risk for falling behind need more, and more varied, support.

The two vignettes that follow illustrate how teachers are reexamining their curricula to respond to both the benefits and the challenges of the standards. One vignette, offering the perspective of a literacy consultant, focuses on how teachers can make sense of the standards themselves and use that understanding to reshape their curricula and their teaching. The second vignette focuses on the way that thoughtful curriculum planning can help to ensure that students will be well prepared to meet standards.

Standards trouble our practice

Linda Eldridge, a literacy consultant to middle-grades language arts teachers in a midwestern state, observes that teachers can benefit most from standards when they use them to "trouble their practice." Linda explains, "Teachers examine the standards carefully. They say, 'If I'm going to have a wonderful language arts program, it will have to have in it all the elements that the standards call for.' Teachers evaluate their own curricula and say, 'I'm really good at addressing this standard, but I don't even know what this other standard means.'"

Linda describes one teacher who determined that she was meeting her state's standard requiring "ideas in action" by involving her students in cross-age projects in the community which connected her students' home and school experiences. "This teacher observed, 'My kids are going out into the community and doing

> "[A teacher] can use rubrics [scoring guides] to beat the band and it's not going to actually help kids understand the skills and concepts called for in the standards unless she thinks about them, really understands them herself, and determines how to apply what she's learned to her teaching."

service. But I'm not teaching the craft of writing as well as I should be. My students' writing is not as good as I want it to be.' So she has started to engage students in a sequence of writing assignments that document their community service efforts. The assignments begin with personal narratives. Students write about their experiences in the community. Then, they move to descriptive, compare/contrast, and cause and effect essays. All of these are required by our state standards. In the essays, her students make the connection between their experiences and significant issues that affect the community. For example, a student who works in a food pantry might write a cause and effect essay that talks about increasing rents and the effect that has on single-income families' abilities to feed and clothe their children."

Linda recalls another teacher who observed, "'It really bothers me that oral language skills are missing from my curriculum. I've got to do some work on that because if I don't, my students won't meet that standard.' Having realized that, this teacher began integrating oral language skills into classroom activities. So I would say that what I see happening is that the standards trouble these teachers' practice."

Linda also describes the tensions created by the simultaneous focus on standards and assessment. "I think the standards call for us to be thoughtful and improve our teaching over a lifetime. But I think the assessments also sometimes leave us running around like chickens with our heads cut off. How do you get teachers to focus on their own learning so that the kids can benefit, when they're so worried about a test? They start to think it's the test that they need to focus on, and that's not entirely the case."

Linda continues, "For example, take learning how to teach the kinds of writing required by the standards. Until a teacher really engages in writing herself, reflects on her own writing, and tries to figure out the implications for kids, whatever she teaches will be fairly superficial. She can use rubrics [scoring guides] to beat the band and it's not going to actually help kids understand the skills and concepts called for in the standards unless she thinks about them, really understands them herself, and determines how to apply what she's learned to her teaching. So there is a tremendous tension, I think, between what the standards are really calling for and the short-term demands of the tests. Right now, I am working on standards-based teaching and learning with a lot of teachers, and one of the things that I've started to say to them right up front is, 'Hey, this *is* overwhelming at first! Whether you're an experienced or a new teacher, this is overwhelming.'"

Nevertheless, Linda concludes that teachers who use the standards to identify the gaps in their curriculum and their students' learning, and then thoughtfully reexamine their curriculum and work to fill those gaps, are improving their teaching. Sometimes this is a matter of making adjustments in an already robust curriculum; often, it involves teachers' questioning and reformulating aspects of their fundamental approach to teaching and learning.

Curriculum planning guided by standards

It takes careful planning for teachers to construct a curriculum that systematically addresses the standards. Larry Carson, an eighth-grade teacher in a suburban district in California, describes the role that standards play in his language arts curriculum planning. "I use a process called 'curriculum mapping.' I sit down in the summer and I look at my district curriculum guide for language arts. I look at the state benchmarks for my grade level, which tell me what the students need to be able to do. I look at the standards. Then I think about the things that I want to accomplish. I ask myself, 'How do they fit in with the standards?'

"I take a big piece of chart paper, and I draw ten boxes. Each box is a month. In each box, I put the theme that I want to explore with students. At the same time, I choose the literature we'll read to accompany the theme or question. For example, I might want students to explore the theme, 'The Characteristics of an Ideal Society.' So I'll choose *The Giver* by Lois Lowry. Our discussions and writing about this novel will center around the 'ideal society' theme. Then I write my specific objectives—all the things I want students to know and be able to do.

"I think about the literature I've chosen and decide which literary elements to teach. I ask myself, 'Will *The Giver* lend itself best to the study of figurative language, theme, mood, or character development?' Then I identify the reading skills and strategies I want students to learn. For example, 'Reciprocal Teaching' is a method that research has shown to be effective in promoting conscious use of reading strategies for improving comprehension. With reciprocal teaching, students learn how to predict, ask questions, clarify, and summarize as they read. Another example is the 'Question-Answer-Response.' With this strategy, kids learn to

"As I map out the curriculum this way, I keep checking the standards and benchmarks to make sure that I've addressed the ones that I'm responsible for."

answer literal and inferential questions. They learn that the answers to some questions are right in the text. Answering other questions requires that they combine information in the text with what they already know. Answering others depends entirely on knowledge they already have.

"Then, depending on the novel, I put in the kind of writing we'll focus on, like narrative or persuasive essays, along with the writing skills and grammar we'll study. For example, I know I'm going to work with my students on how to organize their ideas in their writing, using graphic organizers or semantic maps to help them visually lay out the ideas in the novel and draw the connections between them. In narrative, we might focus on vivid descriptions and voice. I might plan mini-lessons on punctuation or dialogue, or have students work on combining sentences. The specifics may change, of course, as I see what kinds of problems actually come up in students' writing. But as I map out the curriculum this way, I keep checking the standards and benchmarks to make sure that I've addressed the ones that I'm responsible for."

Once he has mapped out the themes and learning objectives, Larry moves on to defining what students will actually do in the classroom. He says, "Then I list the kinds of activities I'll use, like literature circles, large group instruction, or individualized instruction. The activity I use depends on my objectives. For example, if I want all the kids to learn about character or plot, I teach a lesson to the whole class. If a few of them need to work on punctuation, I work with them separately. I often use literature circles, because they provide a format for discussing literature that includes assigned roles for each student so that everyone is expected to get in on discussion of the book. For example, one student might be in charge of vocabulary. Another might direct the discussion, or be the illustrator. There is lots of structure in literature circles. You don't just send students off to discuss the book. They have specific things to accomplish.

"I also have to think about how I will address the range of students I teach. How will I challenge all my students? How will I deal with the individual needs of struggling students? What literature is available for outside reading? Of course, once I've met students and identified their strengths and weaknesses, I'll know better, but I want to start planning it all out early."

A final component of Larry's planning is consideration of how he will assess students' work. He says, "Once I have the plan mapped out, I begin to make up rubrics to match my objectives and the standards. I always tell my students in advance exactly what I want them to know and be able to do, and how I will assess their work.

"So I fill in the boxes in my curriculum map all the way up to June. It's a process that's ongoing. I know that I have goals and I don't always achieve them, and sometimes I get sidetracked. But the map is a very valuable tool. And the standards guide my creation of the map."

A rigorous middle-grades language arts curriculum encourages students to explore novels, poetry, short stories, essays, biographies, and autobiographies. It helps students learn strategies for comprehending and analyzing texts, and gain an understanding that literature can be a vehicle for making sense of human experiences.

What literature should be included in the curriculum? The *Standards for the English Language Arts* recommend that students read contemporary and historical literature that is relevant to their lives. Contemporary selections should reflect the diversity of our society, accurately represent women and minorities, and introduce students to other societies and cultures. The works of artists from past times and cultures should provide students with opportunities to extend their understandings of literary language and devices, and explore the timeless qualities of the human condition.

Experts in developing language arts curriculum suggest that teachers select and organize their literature around important themes—questions and ideas that promote thinking. With regard to the breadth of materials, the quantity should be sufficient to support complex writing and discussion. Too many selections will result in superficial treatment; too few will limit students' experience of genre, style, and substance.

Some of the challenges teachers encounter in making literature selections that balance depth and breadth include:

- Giving struggling readers access to literature that is age-appropriate but may be too difficult for them to read independently.

ACADEMIC RIGOR

What literature will students read, and how will these literature choices balance depth of exploration with breadth of literary experiences?

Experts in developing language arts curriculum suggest that teachers select and organize their literature around important themes—questions and ideas that promote thinking.

- Providing all students with opportunities to choose and read texts at their independent and instructional reading levels, both for pleasure and to further their reading development, when reading levels of the students in a class may vary widely.

- Integrating literature study with learning of language arts skills and processes.

- Accommodating required texts.

- Coordinating with the content focus of other disciplines (most often social studies).

The following vignette illustrates how one teacher uses a theme to guide literature selections that allow her to integrate exploration of important human issues, independent reading and student choice, study of the structure and language of literature, building of vocabulary and other skills, and preparation for standards-based assessment.

Selecting and organizing literature around themes

Joanne Long has been teaching language arts for 31 years in an urban district in the Northeast. She has learned that taking a thematic approach helps her organize a standards-driven curriculum using appropriate literature selections for students who come into her classroom reading at a range of different levels. Using this approach, she is able to integrate district-required books into her curriculum without leaving some students behind or holding others back. Joanne observes, "I have 129 seventh graders. All of them take the state test in the spring. We have heterogeneous grouping in our classes, and the kids' reading levels are all over the place. The district gives us a list of required novels. For example, all the seventh graders are required to read Mildred Taylor's *Let the Circle Be Unbroken*. That's a wonderful book, but not all my students can just pick it up and read it. So I have to deal with that. I used to just read *Circle* aloud in class, chapter by chapter. I think we spent three months on that novel. The kids lost interest in it long before we were finished."

Influenced by a professional development experience, Joanne has changed how she deals with the wide range of reading levels in her diverse classroom. As she describes it, "A couple of years ago, we had a literacy consultant who came to our school once a week and ran workshops for the whole faculty on strategies for meeting the different needs of students in heterogeneous classrooms. She coached us in our classrooms and encouraged us to try new approaches that would make the ideas in the literature we teach accessible to all the kids, yet also focus on building their language skills.

"One of the approaches the consultant encouraged us to try is theme-based instruction. I selected themes that I thought were important and that also would accommodate the novels my district requires for seventh grade. One of the themes I chose was 'connections.' What is it that connects people and families? Why do they stay connected? Why are connections between people important? *Let the Circle Be Unbroken* fits with that theme. I also chose short stories, plays, poems, and nonfiction selections to go with that theme. Our district has a new literature anthology, which has a lot of good selections. I chose 'A Crush' by Cynthia Rylant, the story of a developmentally delayed man who has a crush on a tattooed woman who works in a hardware store. I also chose O. Henry's story 'A Retrieved Reformation,' along with a selection from *The Autobiography of Malcolm X*. I know that some teachers don't like reading excerpts from complete works, but I don't have the time to read the whole book with my kids, so at least they're having an experience with this writing.

"In addition to exploring the theme, I also teach plot, character, setting, and figurative language. We study these in the context of the required reading. First we read the short selections. Then we read *Circle*. That's a pretty difficult novel and not everyone can read it independently. In the past, my objective was just to get them through the novel. Now I really want them to know how to read and analyze literature. So I do a lot of prereading activities to build vocabulary and background knowledge, and connect with what kids already know. Then I begin to read the story to them so I can explain the historical background and get them interested. I let them read in class so I can identify the kids who are having a hard time with the book. I use books on tape, buddy reading (where kids read to each other), and summaries of some of the chapters. I make individual decisions about what sections of the book students are responsible for. We do a lot of discussion and writing about the theme. We look at how it unfolds in *Circle*. The kids compare and contrast relationships and characters in their writing. They work on open-ended responses, like the ones on the state test."

> "In the past, my objective was just to get them through the novel. Now I really want them to know how to read and analyze literature."

Joanne has also devised an outside reading program that supports and extends classroom instruction. "It's really critical for my students to do outside reading, but I don't want them to read just anything. I want them to read for pleasure, but at the same time, there's so much for them to learn. I have to make the most of every assignment. So they read novels outside of class, but we use them in class to study theme and literary devices, and as the basis for writing and literature discussions, along with the required reading." To guide students' independent reading, Joanne uses a resource guide that classifies book titles by theme and reading level. She notes that this enables her to "suggest novels to students that are at a comfortable reading level and are related to the class theme. I give students choices. Some students choose the same novels and work in groups. Others work alone. All of them can read and analyze literature, and discuss and write about the theme.

"When my students took the state test last year, they told me that they were happy when they saw a question about themes. They felt prepared and they did much better on these open-ended questions than students in other years had. They also improved as readers, writers, and thinkers. They may not all be at grade level yet, but they're getting there. I know from the standardized test results that they've made progress. Next year's teachers will have to build on that. Without the common theme, and the reading, writing, and discussions built around it, I couldn't make it work."

EQUITY

How will the curriculum both challenge and support students with diverse social and academic experiences to become skilled, thoughtful readers and communicators?

The current education reform movement seeks to hold all students to high standards of knowledge and performance, and to hold districts, schools, administrators, and teachers accountable for student success. Achieving high standards for all students in our diverse classrooms requires that schools provide students who are vulnerable to falling behind with the kinds of intellectually challenging instruction and learning experiences that are often reserved for the most academically proficient students. In language arts, this means ensuring that all students have access to the intellectual content of contemporary and historical literature of different genres and from different cultures; understand literary language and structures; and develop their skills in reading, writing, and oral language.

Achieving these goals requires that schools transform themselves into cultures in which high expectations for all students are the norm. It also requires that teachers carefully assess student work as they make decisions about learning experiences that will move their students toward fulfilling these expectations. Within this context, language arts curriculum development should begin with standards and assessment, focus on developing students' understanding, and ensure that students are supported by excellent teaching. Teaching should be guided by careful assessment rather than habit or ideology. Teachers should ask: What evidence do we have that students are acquiring critical language arts knowledge and processes? What instructional strategies are available to support individual students who are not progressing toward the standards?

The two vignettes that follow illustrate how two teachers and their school districts combine a challenging curriculum with the kind of ongoing assessment, flexibility in instruction, devotion of extra time and resources, and willingness to be accountable that are required to address the difficult challenge of achieving high standards for all their students.

Those who need more time and resources to meet high standards have them

Joyce Soto teaches English and social studies to a very diverse group of seventh and eighth graders in a large urban district in the Northeast. Her school was created by dividing a large middle school into three smaller schools. Although the three schools are housed in the same large building, each one functions independently.

In Joyce's school, all students are expected to meet the standards for their city, *New Standards™ Student Performance Standards*.[1] According to Joyce, among these standards is the requirement that all students read 25 books each year. By the end of eighth grade, students are also required to create portfolios that provide evidence they can compose a persuasive essay and other essays that demonstrate their ability to interpret, analyze, and evaluate literature. Joyce describes these portfolios as "quite rigorous and kind of daunting. In the sixth and seventh grades we really practice

---

[1] Washington, DC: National Center on Education and the Economy and the University of Pittsburgh, 1997. (See Chapter 4 for a brief description of these standards.)

"We always have the standards in front of kids so that they know what they have to do to meet them. Then, if they fall below or are approaching a particular standard, we give them specific instruction and work with them so they can meet that standard."

doing the portfolio, so that by eighth grade they will all be able to put it together."

Joyce sees that her challenge is to get all students to meet the standards by the end of eighth grade. She uses a scoring system for student work that is tied to the standards and that helps her to focus her teaching. She explains, "A score of one is exceeding the standard, a two is passing, a three is approaching the standard, and a four is falling below the standard. I expect every student to get at least a two. We always have the standards in front of kids so that they know what they have to do to meet them. Then, if they fall below or are approaching a particular standard, we give them specific instruction and work with them so they can meet that standard, but a two, that's the end and everyone has to get there."

Getting all students "there" requires careful planning and hard work. Joyce says, "First of all, I look at what the kids need to know. I look at the standards and say, 'They need to have these five things. And when do we want to do this?' So I map out the whole year by the month. For example, I know that in May we're going to do an 'I-search' [a research process that details the student's search for information, along with the specific information gathered]. I know that we're going to do poetry and really focus on writing our own poetry anthologies in March. I know that we're going to read Mildred Taylor's *Roll of Thunder, Hear My Cry* and Sandra Cisneros's *The House on Mango Street*. It's important for the kids to read well-written literature by authors like these who are 'insiders'—who really know and can write about their cultures. So, I have an idea of where the year is going to go. Then I look at what I want to teach the kids and what they already know. Knowing my kids and what they bring to the classroom really determines what I'm going to teach them. What do they need to know? How can I get them to that point?"

Joyce assesses students' progress toward the standards through ongoing classroom activities including journals, written and oral responses to literature, and "literary letters" in which students write to each other about their reading. She notes that the written responses are "a way that we really assess comprehension. If students write, 'I'm reading this book. It's really good. What are you reading?' I have a pretty good idea that they really don't know what they're reading. I want them to be getting into some deeper issues, looking at characters, plot, and author's craft.

With responses to literature, as you're assessing their reading you're also assessing their writing."

Joyce describes her students as "mostly struggling with their reading, kids who are really in need of specific skills and strategies in order to become better readers and meet the standards. Students who have fallen below the 50th percentile in reading scores are enrolled in an after-school, extended-day literacy program, which is six extra hours of reading a week for kids."

In this after-school program, Joyce explains, "I basically do a reading workshop. I do a lot of conferring with individual kids. I have about eleven kids in the class; usually about eight show up. They come for an hour before school and two hours after school, two days a week. I give them one-on-one instruction and one-on-one attention and more time to process, more time to read. We do responses. Kids read and write or discuss the ideas and emotions the literature evokes for them. We do a lot of shared reading. I read to the kids while they follow along. I model reading strategies as I read. Kids also read independently at least a half-hour each day. I have sets of books at their reading levels—books that are interesting but that they can manage on their own. I try to reinforce what we do in the classroom with the rest of the kids. But I also give them a chance to read to me one on one and work individually on the decoding and comprehension strategies that they need."

When asked about the impact of standards on her diverse student population, Joyce responded, "One of the nice things about standards and one of the not-so-nice things is that there *is* a standard. We can't say, 'This is really good work for John because he's never in school. And you know, golly, he's really trying.' Either he meets the standard or he doesn't meet the standard. And so, in a way, our hands are tied. He's so far below. But then we know what work we have to do to try to catch him up. So I think the ways that we assess the kids have to be the same according to *New Standards*."

Joyce designs her curriculum around *New Standards* and works hard to assure that all her students meet them. She is supported by a school culture that holds high expectations for all. Within this context, student work and assessment are at the center of teaching and learning. For Joyce, equity does not mean that all students are treated in the same way. Instruction and resources

"Students who have fallen below the 50th percentile in reading scores are enrolled in an after-school, extended-day literacy program, which is six extra hours of reading a week for kids."

differ; pacing varies as well. Joyce's description of the after-school workshop for struggling readers suggests the kinds of demands on teachers' time and school resources that such a commitment to equity can entail. However, since the goals are the same for all students, those who need more time and resources to meet high standards have them.

All kids can learn, but on different days at different rates

Abby Stevens is a seventh-grade teacher at Diego Rivera Middle School, which is located in a medium-sized, southwestern city. The majority of her students are Latino/a or African American, and most qualify for free or reduced-price lunch. As in many other communities, Abby's district has placed a high priority on students' meeting academic standards. Student progress is measured each year with the state test which, Abby says, "addresses all of the skills that students must have to pass a particular grade level. If they don't pass the test on those skills, they are not allowed to pass that grade level. There is no such thing as social promotion." Teachers in this middle school feel accountable for student learning. Abby notes that "the motto of our school is 'All kids can learn, but on different days at different rates.' We don't believe that if we give a quiz today everybody has to make 100 on it and then we just move onto the next one, and okay, that's finished. And if you made a 50 percent, too bad, you just didn't listen! That 'only one chance' approach is totally against what we believe."

Abby explains that her students have multiple opportunities to demonstrate that they have met a particular standard. "If for some reason a student doesn't work well within the classroom setting, then we have a 'Standards Lab.' Students are allowed to go to the lab after school and try to complete that standard with a different teacher. Perhaps the student is just not on the same wavelength as the classroom teacher. So now she or he gets to work with a different teacher, and still try to accomplish that standard before the school year is over. Our job is to teach students whatever they need to meet the standards."

In 1995, Abby reports, the district was ready to "shut the school down for failing test scores. Students at Rivera had failed state tests for three years in a row in all subjects." Since that time, a number of changes have taken place and, according to Abby,

Rivera "is now a recognized school, which means that 70 percent of all the students are scoring at least 80 percent on the assessments." These changes include block scheduling—which gives teachers longer class periods with students—and the "creation of 'houses' in which students have one teacher for language arts and social studies, and one teacher for math and science." Abby believes that the block scheduling and house system enable teachers to get to know students better. "In this environment," she says, "it's easier to provide ongoing assessment of student progress."

In her classroom, Abby focuses on bringing all students to high standards, regardless of their previous levels of achievement or cultural and linguistic backgrounds. The learning objectives and expectations for students are clear, Abby reports. "We have a learning map in the classroom, which is a road map of where we are going, what we will learn. This map tells the students exactly what we expect to accomplish. Every week, we review this map to be sure that students know where we are headed." To make the expectations even more explicit, Abby gives students rubrics—scoring guides that articulate the components of successful performance on particular tasks.

If an individual student doesn't meet these expectations, Abby believes that it is her responsibility "to reassess a student's needs, and try to address those needs better, because whatever we did just didn't work the first time. If we taught something orally and a student doesn't pass, we'll teach it a different way. Then we'll reassess."

Because students must demonstrate their knowledge on the state test through reading and writing tasks, Abby provides numerous opportunities for students to practice test-taking skills. She says, "This allows them to really demonstrate what they have learned in language arts. I give written tests that consist of several different formats, like multiple choice, short essay, fill in the blanks, or true and false. It could be any of those things, but it's always at least three different formats within one test."

While she knows that raising student achievement on the state test is critical, Abby worries that the emphasis on assessment in the district may limit her curriculum. "We spend so much time getting the kids ready for the state test. That's important, but we don't seem to have enough time for other important things like

If an individual student doesn't meet these expectations, Abby believes that it is her responsibility "to reassess a student's needs, and try to address those needs better, because whatever we did just didn't work the first time."

reading novels and plays and poetry. I want my students to love literature. I want them to be able to put their ideas and feelings down on paper. I want them to use reading and writing to help them understand themselves. But I always have to be thinking about the test. When I go to meetings with other language arts teachers in my district, we talk about this a lot. It's a real dilemma."

Within the constraints of the state test, Abby does find some room to focus on other aspects of learning that she believes are important. For example, in addition to ongoing assessment of students' reading and writing, Abby also builds in opportunities for students to demonstrate their learning with hands-on activities. "I think that it's the best of both worlds, because in the written test, I am testing the knowledge that I said you had to have. The hands-on activity allows students the opportunity to show me what they learned that they found interesting, in addition to what I required from them. So, if you are that wonderful artist, or if you are that wonderful musician, or if you are that wonderful actor, then you get to perform in your strength. I think everybody becomes a winner in that situation."

DEVELOPMENTAL APPROPRIATENESS

How will the curriculum ensure that the study of language arts is engaging, motivating, and suitably challenging for middle-grades students?

Making the language arts curriculum developmentally appropriate for middle-grades students requires a general understanding of ways to engage learners and knowledge of the particular developmental characteristics of young adolescents. A developmentally appropriate curriculum:

- Builds on students' existing knowledge and current levels of understanding.
- Connects with everyday issues of interest to middle-grades students.
- Engages students in literacy activities that have a genuine communicative purpose.
- Offers opportunities for peer discussion and collaboration through activities that capitalize on the social nature of middle-grades students.

These aspects of the curriculum should combine to promote students' intellectual and skills development. That is, it is not sufficient for students to be engaged in personally meaningful activities; these activities need to be carefully designed to foster students' growth in the reading, writing, and oral language competencies as laid out in the academic standards.

The following two vignettes illustrate different approaches to making the curriculum both rigorous and developmentally appropriate. In one approach, students participate in a series of experiences that give them access to a historical text through reading, writing, listening, research, drama, art, and oral presentations. In the other approach, students use material from their own lives as the focus for an equally carefully organized set of literacy experiences. While these two approaches differ markedly in some respects, both take advantage of students' interests, experiences, and growing cognitive and social capacities to engage them in learning that challenges them intellectually and builds their skills. Both use what teachers know about their students to carefully structure the curriculum so that students develop the literacy knowledge and skills required by the standards and engage in increasingly sophisticated forms of reading, writing, and use of oral language. In fact, the two approaches are not mutually exclusive; that is, a high-quality language arts curriculum might combine elements of both.

Using art and drama to open doors to the intellectual content of the curriculum

Susan Olsen and Barry Holman teach sixth-grade language arts in a middle school in the Northeast. The two work closely together in planning and implementing the sixth-grade language arts curriculum, with its combination of contemporary and historical literature. Over the course of the school year, students study the characters in the novels *Call It Courage, Julie of the Wolves,* and *A Christmas Carol* to understand how individuals develop and change over time as a result of their experiences.

According to Susan and Barry, each year some of their students have great difficulty reading Charles Dickens's *A Christmas Carol,* a book that is required reading for sixth grade in their district. Susan reports, "In past years, it didn't seem that all the kids were getting it. It was too difficult for them to read the original Dickens version. And it didn't seem relevant to them at all." The two teachers met with Martha Wright, a literacy consultant with whom they had been working for several years. Their goal was to identify ways they could help these modern American students understand the Victorian language and setting of the novel and connect with its characters, issues, and themes.

Susan describes how she and Barry changed the study of *A Christmas Carol.* "From our work with Martha, we knew that we had to do a lot with building students' background knowledge. So we spent quite a bit of time talking about Dickens and what life was like in Victorian England. Then we got the kids involved in a wonderful project. Barry and I did this together, with all our students. We created a walking tour of Dickens's London. Sixth graders love hands-on projects. Several of the kids volunteered to come after school for many, many hours, to construct a life-sized set of Victorian London. They painted what the streets of London would have looked like—narrow, cobblestoned, dark, cold, foggy—all of the terms Dickens used in the story. We consulted the book very carefully for that. We also did some research about Dickens, Victorian London, and how his books were social commentaries.

"Once the set was built, we did the walking tour. There were five stops on the tour. The volunteers who constructed the sets became tour guides, and they dressed in costumes and acted as if they were in that time period. Each of them would lead a small group of kids from one stop to the next. At each of these stops there were different activities going on. At one stop, there was a teacher dressed up as Charles Dickens. He talked about his background, his family life, and working at the blacking factory as a child. The kids were able to ask him questions. Then they would move to another stop where a teacher, dressed in a period costume, acted the part of Mrs. Cratchit and explained some of the traditions of a poor Victorian family. She made a Christmas pudding and the kids tasted it. The kids loved that.

"Three of the other stops were scenes from the novel that we weren't sure that the kids would completely understand. So we had teachers and seventh-grade volunteers help us by acting out some of the major scenes from the novel. Then each of the actors explained, 'This is who I was. This is what Dickens was trying to say through my character.' And the kids could ask questions of the actors.

"The logistics weren't easy. It was a very tricky schedule. Half of the group, about 100 kids, were going through the stations. We had the other 100 kids learning period dancing and acting out the Feziwig ballroom dancing scene in the gym. With sixth graders, it's important to give them lots of opportunities to move around. The dancing was a little silly, but they enjoyed it." Susan acknowledges that planning and orchestrating the walking tour was "a major effort," but she believes "it was worthwhile to give students access to the language, setting, and characters in the novel."

With the tour as a jumping-off point, the teachers found ways to immerse students in the language of the novel and take advantage of their eagerness to dramatize the characters and events in order to develop their understanding of character, narrative structure, and theme. As Susan explains, "One of the reasons we have to read *A Christmas Carol* is so that kids can study language and see how different the English language was in the Victorian period. But you don't have to read all of *A Christmas Carol* to do that. We showed the movie and did a plot chart, so that all students understood the setting, rising action, falling action, and climax. Our theme for the year is 'Journey of Change.' Scrooge is a great example of a character who makes that journey, so we placed a particular emphasis on character development. Whether the kids were ready to read the book on their own or not, they all learned the literary elements.

"We also had students doing work in groups. We divided the book into sections, and each group had to do a 'scene study' of one of these sections. They had to become the characters. They had to understand Dickens's language well enough to turn the prose into a script, and then they acted out their parts, calling on their oral presentation skills. We have been working hard to integrate oral presentation into our curriculum, since it's part of the state standards. We spent several classes discussing body language, movement, voice, and projection. Ultimately, each group acted out their scene in front of both classes.

"Next, students wrote an analysis of their character and how that character contributed to Scrooge's journey of change. So, again, they were looking carefully at character development, not just of the protagonist, but of all the characters who influenced Scrooge."

Susan adds that she and Barry work hard to develop strategies that will enable even students who struggle to read the novel to participate fully in the study of the novel's characters and theme. But she stresses that they also continue to work with these students to improve their reading skills. At the same time, she and

"We divided the book into sections, and each group had to do a 'scene study' of one of these sections. They had to become the characters. They had to understand Dickens's language well enough to turn the prose into a script, and then they acted out their parts, calling on their oral presentation skills."

"The idea was to have kids use reading and writing to make a positive difference in their community. Kids identify a health-related problem in their community or in their lives, and then they use their reading and writing skills to change that."

Barry believe that efforts to help these students to read fluently at grade level should not preclude opportunities for the students' intellectual engagement and growth.

Susan and Barry both conclude that the additional time and effort they put into planning and implementing the study of *A Christmas Carol* "was well worth it." Their concern about meeting the developmental needs of their sixth graders led to the creation of a unit that integrated the language, performing, and visual arts, and gave all of their students access to the intellectual content of the novel. Through activities and explorations that intrigued and engaged students as well as challenged them intellectually, the curriculum unit developed students' literacy skills, including analytic writing, dramatic writing, and oral presentation. The unit also built students' knowledge of literary concepts, including narrative structure, character development, and theme.

Making students' lives the material for literacy learning

Therese Connor is a 26-year veteran teacher in an economically depressed city in the Midwest. She is an active member of the National Council of Teachers of English, and has participated in the National Writing Project for many years. She has published articles about language arts education, and has collaborated with language arts educators at the national, state, and local levels.

Therese believes strongly that middle-grades language arts instruction must be directly connected to the lives of her students, whose out-of-school literacy experiences can vary greatly from those in school. She uses the skills, knowledge, and experiences that students bring to the classroom as the starting points for teaching and learning.

Through her involvement with the National Writing Project and experience working with several university researchers, Therese participated in a grant-funded project that allowed her to make her language arts curriculum more relevant and meaningful to her middle-grades students. Therese describes this collaborative curriculum effort. "The idea was to have kids use reading and writing to make a positive difference in their community. Kids identify a health-related problem in their community or in their lives, and then they use their reading and writing skills to change that. We had teachers in three different states working on this. So teachers had a network of other teachers interested in helping kids to see the connection between their writing and their reading, and to see themselves as important members of their communities. What we realized early on was that just about everything is a health issue. If it isn't a physical health issue, it's an emotional health issue. That was something that was kind of a jolt to all of us. Everything emerged as a health issue for the urban students we teach."

Therese describes how the focus on health-related community concerns influenced her own curriculum. "Each of the teachers who've participated in this project has implemented the idea in somewhat different ways. With my seventh graders, I looked for readings that focused on issues about growing up. Some of the books we're reading are *Dragon's Gate, The House on Mango Street,* and *Roll of Thunder, Hear My Cry.* I also did a read-aloud of *The Outsiders* this fall. I start out just trying to get the kids doing their own reading and their own writing. They write letters to each other, back and forth, about what they're reading.

"Now we're about halfway through the year, and we're reading *The House on Mango Street* which is composed of a series of vignettes. The students are very involved in it right now, and they're writing vignettes of their own. They've written four vignettes so far and revised two of them for final drafts. This week they started work on a fifth one. We read one of the vignettes from the novel—a conversation between two girls written entirely in dialogue. The two girls start talking about benign things, like different names for clouds and for snow. Then all of a sudden they start taking digs at each other, and before you know it, they're exchanging insults and threatening not to be friends anymore. I love it because it's so typical of what can happen to pre-adolescent and adolescent kids. One moment someone's your best friend and the next moment you can't stand her.

"After we'd done some prereading activities, and I read the vignette and we discussed it, I said to them, 'Think back to a conversation that you had with a friend when something that was said was misunderstood by one of you, and the conversation took a bad turn, so that by the end of the conversation you really didn't feel the same about each other.' Most of them said, 'Yes, yes,' they'd had this experience. They could picture it in their heads. My goal was to try to get them to put some dialogue down on paper, because they haven't tried this so far. So I did a mini-lesson teaching everybody about how to write dialogue."

"They were really motivated to write well and correct the spelling and the mechanics because they wanted other girls to get the information they were communicating."

Therese explains that she had two objectives in this assignment: "to introduce the conventions of dialogue as far as indenting and so forth, and to focus on writing dialogue that's real. I thought that if they could imagine something that really happened, and if they could put that down on paper, that would be a good start for writing real dialogue." Therese also thought that this writing assignment would get students interested in analyzing why the vignette from *The House on Mango Street* seemed so real.

She reports that students "had a hard time telling the story all in dialogue. They wanted to say things like, 'Once upon a time,' or 'One day my friend and I were talking.' So my student teacher and I spent about half an hour conferencing with individual kids. We did that in class and got a good start. And then I asked them to take the draft home and work on it. We'll come back to the writing in the next class."

Therese continues, "That's an example of how we use the literature as a springboard to get students thinking and writing about issues they're facing in their lives; in this case, conflict with friends, which can sometimes escalate into violence. We've also used these issues as the material for research projects. Doing a research paper is required in our state standards." When her students write about their lives, Therese reads their work and helps them learn to identify themes that seem to emerge. She says, "Some kids talk about sibling rivalry. Others talk about parents who have cancer. There's asthma. I had so many kids with inhalers one year, I couldn't believe it. We also learned that our community has the highest number of AIDS cases in the state, and several kids had been directly affected—had friends, a cousin, a father who had died of AIDS. It is very real to them."

Therese notes that her curriculum helps her students connect their mastery of literacy skills to efforts to improve the health of their community. One of the issues that comes up frequently, she notes, is that of teen pregnancy—"older sisters and friends who had babies, for example. Two years ago one group of girls did some research on the rate of teen pregnancy in our area. They interviewed people in the community; they did research on the Internet. And they did a lot of writing about teen pregnancy because it's something that they cared about. They ended up publishing a booklet for other teenage girls based on their research. They were really motivated to write well and correct the spelling and the mechanics because they wanted other girls to get the information they were communicating."

Planning and implementing a rigorous, equitable, and developmentally appropriate language arts curriculum is challenging. Teachers need significant support in learning to meet this challenge. Ongoing professional development must provide educators with:

- Experience in the kinds of intellectually demanding literacy activities their students will engage in.

- A broad and deep knowledge of literature.

- An understanding of how young adolescents develop language arts concepts, skills, and processes.

- Knowledge of teaching strategies that will foster high achievement and facility in using them.

- Familiarity with the kinds of assessments that will help them match instruction to students' needs.

- Access to teaching and learning materials and resources that can help them support all students in meeting the language arts standards.

Districts can support teachers in the following ways:

- Providing workshops and courses that address teachers' needs.

- Allowing time for collaborative planning and for study groups to share and reflect on their experiences and learn from one another.

- Supplying resources including professional literature, videotapes, instructional materials and their accompanying teacher's guides, and a wide range of fiction and nonfiction books.

- Encouraging and providing resources for teachers to take advantage of professional development opportunities beyond the district, such as those offered by the National Writing Project, colleges and universities, and professional organizations.

Teachers and teacher leaders experienced in planning and implementing standards-based curricula highlight several elements they look for in effective professional development. These fall into two

PROFESSIONAL DEVELOPMENT

What will enable educators to plan and implement standards-based language arts curricula, and how can districts support professional development?

If teachers are going to engage students in "curricular conversations" about important ideas, they need to experience such conversations themselves and have the opportunity to reflect on how these experiences can translate into instructional practice.

main categories: formal professional development opportunities and ongoing support.

Formal professional development introduces teachers to new ideas about teaching and learning and new curriculum approaches, and gives them time to explore and reflect on these ideas and approaches. Formal professional development experiences are effective when they:

- Engage teachers in the same kind of work they expect of students in language arts classes (e.g., active reading, discussing, and writing about literature; developing and communicating ideas through reflection, discussion, writing, revision, and editing; integrating the learning and practice of language skills with meaningful communication). If teachers are going to engage students in "curricular conversations" about important ideas, they need to experience such conversations themselves and have the opportunity to reflect on how these experiences can translate into instructional practice.

- Support teachers in making the significant shift from the traditional instructional approach of conveying information (e.g., the theme of a story or the rules for grammar and syntax) to engaging students in active interpretation, discussion, and effective and accurate communication of their ideas.

- Bring teachers who have successfully used standards-based curriculum approaches and materials together with teachers learning to use them.

- Introduce teachers to high-quality materials that can support standards-based teaching and learning and reduce the need for teachers to "reinvent the wheel."

Ongoing support is a second essential component of effective professional development. Teachers using new curriculum approaches benefit from opportunities to learn from those experienced with these approaches, as well as those who, like them, are learning to use the approaches. Such support, whether through visiting coaches, online or telephone conversations, peer consultation, or regular meetings of study groups, offers teachers help in solving problems as they come up. Effective ongoing support provides opportunities for teachers to:

- Access others who are experienced in using the curriculum approaches and materials.

- Share challenges and successes with other colleagues who are using the curriculum approaches and materials.

- Learn to develop and use rubrics (scoring guides), evaluate examples of student work, and use assessments to guide teaching and learning.

Professional development for planning and implementing standards-based curricula is multifaceted. The following two vignettes show how teachers benefit from a coordinated approach to professional development and illustrate a number of different facets of effective professional development. Both vignettes provide examples of how teachers and districts can take advantage of national professional development resources to create local programs that exemplify the features of effective professional development described above. Nationally available programs such as *Junior Great Books, Reading for Real,* and *6 + 1 Traits™ of Writing* are widely recognized for their success in promoting students' reading, writing, and thinking. *Reading for Real* is highlighted in the first vignette as an example of such programs, several of which are described briefly in Chapter 4 of this guide. The second vignette focuses on the National Writing Project, which has influenced the teaching of writing at all levels over the past quarter century. Many local and regional organizations, including colleges and universities and professional associations, also offer professional development and networking opportunities similar to those provided by the National Writing Project.

A coordinated approach to curriculum and professional development

Angela Santos is a curriculum specialist in a small southeastern city. Her district has adopted Yale University educator James Comer's School Development Program as a vehicle for school improvement. Santos explains, "One of the Comer advisors introduced *Reading for Real* to our district. We were able to fund both the purchase of materials and professional development training through Title VI, which supports innovative programs. We consider *Reading for Real* a very innovative program."

Reading for Real is a literature-based language arts and professional development program aimed at building literacy skills and promoting the academic, social, and emotional development of students in grades 4-8. It is structured around literature that addresses important questions likely to promote complex writing and discussion. (For example, the teacher's guide that accompanies Lois Lowry's *The Giver* focuses on questions such as "What is an ideal society?" and "What does it mean for a person or institution to have authority?") The program includes shared reading (the teacher reads to students), partner reading (students work in pairs), and a family involvement component. Support includes teacher's guides that suggest activities for oral language, reading, and writing. Additionally, extensive professional development opportunities are available, including weeklong courses, videotapes, and on-site consultation.

Angela explains that *Reading for Real* reflects what research shows about effective strategies for improving students' reading and writing. "I have to say that when I first heard about this program, I was skeptical. I hate guides; they're so structured. But *Reading for Real* does just enough. There are no mobiles, no dioramas for students to make. It teaches what real readers do. After you read a book, what do you do? You recommend it to a friend. So *Reading for Real* focuses on the really important things: talking about the books, exploring their themes, learning about new words and new ideas, writing to respond and to understand, making connections and experiencing different perspectives. All the research shows that reading more helps spelling and helps improve vocabulary. The more you read, the better writer you become. The program really lets kids enjoy good books. But it also does give you tools, such as Venn diagrams, to help students organize their thoughts. And the professional development gave us experience in using these tools."

Angela describes the initial phase of professional development for the first group of six teachers in her district who used *Reading for Real* and were then trained to become teacher leaders in their schools. "Over the course of the first couple of years, staff from the Developmental Studies Center [the developers of *Reading for Real*] came to our system several times and did professional development sessions with teachers. In addition to this in-district training, we had access to videotapes that Developmental Studies produced. The videotapes have great examples of teachers implementing strategies for reading, questioning, and writing. That was very helpful. Then in the summer six of us went out to Developmental Studies in California for a week to receive training. The training was very good, and it was intensive. We went eight hours a day and had homework every night. We read the books and did the activities and writing ourselves. Then we got to think and talk about how to use them in our classrooms. We also talked about the videotapes and learned a lot about the questioning process and effective questioning techniques. We also learned how to build learning communities and help students discuss with each other, rather than talking to the teacher all the time.

"When we were out in California, the developers also gave us a very good manual to guide us in working with other teachers. We went through the manual and practiced ways to introduce the program to new teachers and to support continuing teachers. When we came back to the district, we did several professional development sessions with new teachers. We ended up with two teacher leaders in each school who are in charge of the program, and help the other teachers. All of us are now experienced with *Reading for Real* and are able to help other teachers who are struggling with some aspects of the program."

Angela also reports that the teachers who are using the program continue to meet to discuss reading selections, strategies for teaching, and effective ways to integrate the program into the whole middle-grades curriculum. "We have a really diverse population of kids, and *Reading for Real* has a wide range of selections. We take a lot of time to make our selections. We read and discuss them before we actually make a commitment to use them, and eventually the whole grade level decides which books to use. Also, we look for ways to connect the reading selections to other components of the middle-grades curriculum. In fact, we've added nonfiction books so that we can relate the readings more easily to the social studies curriculum, while we are teaching kids about nonfiction as a genre. For example, there's one book we use when students are studying presidential politics. We look for those kinds of connections.

"Also, if a book doesn't work, we try to analyze why. We may decide not to use it again, or we might change the grade level when we use it. We also look at the kids' writing, and share scoring guides and strategies for working with kids on their writing."

Looking back on the district's experience with *Reading for Real*, Angela notes that the schools that initially elected to use the program were schools that had a high percentage of low-achieving students. "We were really in search of something to assist us. And

> **"I realized that the way to bring my students into the world of writers is for me to be a writer and to model writing. . . . I have to understand and use the writing process myself if I'm ever going to be able to teach it to my students."**

our scores have increased—those schools are not low-achieving schools any more. I can't say that *Reading for Real* is the only reason for that, because there are other things going on in these schools, but I feel pretty sure it's a factor. And the professional development and support that went along with the curriculum have had a big impact."

Professional communities and ongoing learning opportunities

"The biggest influence on how I teach is my being a part of the National Writing Project. I think that has had the greatest impact on how I shape my classroom and how I address student learning," says Lois Allen Wills, who has taught fourth through eighth grade language arts for over 20 years in a small rural district in the South. Lois is currently spending a year working with teachers across the district as part of a National Writing Project secondary literacy initiative based at a nearby state university, but will then return to her middle-grades classroom.

The National Writing Project, which was founded in 1974, endures in over 150 sites across the country. It has two key elements: (1) bringing teachers together to write themselves and learn to improve their teaching of writing, and (2) building local capacity to replicate this model.

Lois's experience, of being first a participant in National Writing Project institutes and then a teacher leader herself, is typical. She credits her 15-year involvement in the National Writing Project for inspiring her both as a writer and a teacher. "I started to see myself as a writer, and started reading and hearing writer-educators like Don Graves and Don Murray. Through the mentoring I received, I realized that the way to bring my students into the world of writers is for me to be a writer and to model writing. Five years ago, I was a Fellow for the National Writing Project at the state university. That experience was encouraging. I came to understand that I am responsible for my own professional development. If I become a better reader and writer, and model this for my students, they are likely to do the same. I have to understand and use the writing process myself if I'm ever going to be able to teach it to my students."

Lois reports that her National Writing Project experiences have also encouraged her to create an ongoing study group in her own school. In keeping with the National Writing Project philosophy, members of this group participate together in reading, writing, and discussion, and also consider how to improve the teaching of language arts in their school. Lois talks about the evolution of the group, and how it prompted an initiative to increase parents' involvement in their children's literacy education.

"One of the things that I did in my own school during the first year of this research project was that I got permission from my principal to have an after-school gathering for professional development; I called it 'Professional Conversations.' I did that every week after school, once a week, and just had an open door, served snacks, and invited people to come and talk. We read a shared text, and we had a discussion. We read selections by authors like Lucy Calkins, Don Graves, Nancie Atwell, and Lisa Delpit. What emerged from those conversations was that we really need to focus on doing a better job of teaching writing. We need to teach revision. We need to teach skills explicitly and give students opportunities to practice them in the context of their writing. We also decided that parents are very important, because we only have the kids for six hours a day. The kids are with their families and their own communities for hundreds of hours every year. So we need to make better connections with parents to help them find ways to further support their kids' writing. It's not easy to do this in middle school. Kids don't usually want parents around. So we had to find creative ways to get parents involved.

"As a result of those discussions, I've started doing some things to connect better with parents, and I have better relationships with parents now than I have ever had in all of the years that I've taught. One thing I've done is to videotape what's happening in my classroom and send it home with a journal in which parents respond to what they see happening in my classroom. That has increased the trust level from parents. It's also allowed parents to have input and to help me understand their kids better. Sometimes they see things on the videos that I don't see, and they ask me questions that help me to see new ways to approach students. Or they'll write a response in the journal about their child that will help me to understand something about what the child may or may not have done in their writing or their oral presentation. Students also get to see their parents in new ways—as collaborators, writers, partners with teachers. Through the National Writing Project, I'm also learning about other parent involvement

Lois reports that her National Writing Project experiences have also encouraged her to create an ongoing study group in her own school. . . . Members of this group participate together in reading, writing, and discussion, and also consider how to improve the teaching of language arts in their school.

efforts. The National Writing Project has over 40 programs to create partnerships with parents to benefit their kids."

The parent involvement resources are just one example of the way the National Writing Project connects teachers to sources of information and colleagues around the country that can supplement local professional development resources. Lois notes, "The National Writing Project gives you access to all kinds of resources you wouldn't necessarily have just from your own school or district. This year I'm on a National Writing Project online mailing list that identifies promising websites, and the teachers I'm working with are trying some of these out with their kids. I just keep growing and learning as a writer and a teacher, and I see that happening for other teachers as well, and for the kids with their writing."

Authors Mentioned

The following books are examples of works by the authors that are mentioned by teachers in the vignettes in this chapter.

Atwell, Nancie, *In the Middle: New Understandings About Writing, Reading, and Learning* (Portsmouth, NH: Heinemann, 1987, 1998).

Beane, James (Ed.), *Toward a Coherent Curriculum: 1995 Yearbook of the Association for Supervision and Curriculum Development* (Alexandria, VA: Association for Supervision and Curriculum Development, 1995).

Calkins, Lucy McCormick, *The Art of Teaching Writing* (Portsmouth, NH: Heinemann, 1986, 1994).

Delpit, Lisa D., *Other People's Children: Cultural Conflict in the Classroom* (New York: The New Press, 1995).

Graves, Donald H., *Bring Life into Learning: Create a Lasting Literacy* (Portsmouth, NH: Heinemann, 1999).

Murray, Donald M., *Expecting the Unexpected: Teaching Myself—and Others—to Read and Write* (Portsmouth, NH: Heinemann, 1989).

CHAPTER 2

Curriculum Profiles

When we asked language arts educators in urban, suburban, and rural schools about the questions posed in Chapter 1, several themes emerged in their responses. These include integrating the language arts, organizing the curriculum around themes, using ongoing assessment to guide instruction, and teaching skills. Teachers also painted a graphic picture of the challenges they face every day: How to provide developmentally appropriate instruction to students with a wide range of reading and writing abilities? How to support very diverse students in meeting the same standards? How to engage students in language experiences with genuine purposes and audiences, build on the knowledge students bring from their homes and communities, and provide increasingly more complex literacy experiences over the grades? Many of these challenges are most acute for teachers in high-poverty schools, but teachers in a variety of communities reported teaching as many as 150 or 160 students a day and needing to help a wide range of students meet newly heightened expectations.

Several teachers asked us to provide them with a concrete example of a standards-based language arts curriculum that addresses the questions we have posed. This chapter provides two such concrete examples, which we refer to as curriculum profiles. The first, developed by the sixth-grade language arts faculty at a middle school in the Northeast, is a "working" curriculum that is frequently evaluated and revised by the teachers who use it. The second profile is one that we developed as an example of a curriculum that extends across the middle grades. This profile is based on our interviews with language arts educators, along with our reading of research on language arts and curriculum development.

Both curriculum profiles consist of complex and interrelated information. This information is presented in tables to permit examination of each of the language arts strands separately as well as in conjunction with the others. Although the profiles share a similar format, their content differs somewhat. The first features literature, writing, and language study—primarily grammar, spelling, and vocabulary. The language arts are integrated as students use reading, writing, and a moderate amount of oral language to explore the theme, "Creating one's identity is a journey of self-discovery and change."

The second profile closely follows the *New Standards™ Student Performance Standards* and is organized around reading and literature, writing, and oral language and viewing. Conventions, grammar, and usage are addressed in the context of a focus on the writing. As in the first profile, the language arts are integrated and students engage in complex oral and written conversations. In addition, the substance of these conversations, the "big ideas," are aligned with several of the middle-grades themes suggested by the *Curriculum Standards for Social Studies* published by the National Council for the Social Studies. Thus, this profile provides an example of how language arts and social studies can be integrated.

A Curriculum in Progress for Grade Six

The great majority of the students at Ralph Waldo Emerson Middle School[1] go on to the regional high school and then to four-year colleges. Emerson Middle School's philosophy stresses "a balance of rigorous academics and a nurturing atmosphere that meets the needs of developing adolescents."

The sixth-grade faculty at Emerson have participated in professional development on content area literacy and understand that students must read widely and extensively to build their vocabulary and background knowledge. They have developed a "reading across the curriculum" program that begins in September when students read a work of fiction for language arts class. As the year progresses, students read biography, nonfiction, and fiction for social studies and science classes; selections that require logic and

---

[1] This is a pseudonym.

problem-solving skills for mathematics class; and books that deal with adolescent social issues for guidance courses.

While literature has become a component of all the content areas at Emerson, it is at the center of the language arts curriculum. Through literature, students explore concepts and ideas that help them make sense of human experiences. The sixth-grade language arts curriculum focuses on a yearlong theme: "Creating one's identity is a journey of self-discovery and change." Students spend much of the year reading, discussing, and writing about literature that explores this theme, including *Call it Courage, A Christmas Carol,* and *Julie of the Wolves.*[2] For the most part, specific language arts skills are taught in the context of theme-related activities.

Emerson's language arts curriculum is carefully reviewed throughout the year. It is "a work in progress" and is modified and adjusted to ensure that it focuses on promoting the knowledge and skills required by the state and district standards. Key elements of this sixth-grade curriculum are identified in the table that follows. Brief definitions of terms that may be unfamiliar follow the first occurrence of each term. These terms are printed in boldface.

---

[2]The vignette in Chapter 1 describing the walking tour of Victorian London elaborates one unit from Emerson's sixth-grade curriculum.

Grade Six Curriculum

Theme: Creating one's identity is a journey of self-discovery and change

Literature	Writing	Language Study	Additional Information
Unit One: Introductions Students read self-selected fiction.	• Assess all incoming students' writing. • Introduce students to the **writing process**. (The writing process involves several recursive activities including planning, drafting, revising, and editing.) • Introduce expository writing with a descriptive essay based on a group camping experience.	• Introduce the parts of speech through the expository writing assignment.	All sixth-grade students attend a three-day camping/team-building program at the beginning of the year. Teachers use **rubrics** to assess student performance. (Rubrics are scoring guides that articulate criteria for evaluating student work.)
Unit Two: Call It Courage Students read *Call It Courage* by Armstrong Sperry. Focus on: • plot structure • theme: the journey of change	• Writing about theme. • Instruction on topic sentence, use of details to support assertions, concluding sentence. • Instruction on transitional sentences.	• **Mini-lessons** on usage as it relates to students' writing. (A mini-lesson is a 5- to 10-minute lesson during which explicit instruction is provided in a specific skill or strategy.) • Vocabulary from *Call It Courage* related to theme.	*Call it Courage* is the story of how a young Polynesian boy conquers his fear of the sea.

Grade Six Curriculum (continued)

Literature	Writing	Language Study	Additional Information
Unit Three: A Christmas Carol Students read *A Christmas Carol* by Charles Dickens. Focus on: • background on Victorian England • background on Charles Dickens • plot structure • character development • mood • language of Dickens	• Continued work on expository essay structure. • Introduction to responding to open-ended questions similar to those on the state assessment. • Students write an expository essay on the subject, "Scrooge and the Journey of Change." • Students write a narrative holiday memory essay based on an interview (see "Language Study"); focus on setting, plot, character, mood; ties are made to *A Christmas Carol.* • Instruction on using dialogue in narrative. • Instruction on revision.	• Instruction on conducting interviews. • Students interview a family member about holiday memories. • Vocabulary from *A Christmas Carol.* • Walking tour of Dickens's London.	One of the objectives in using this text is to introduce the language of Dickens. This language is difficult for many students. To familiarize them with the language and to build their knowledge of plot, character, and setting, the film version of *A Christmas Carol* is shown before students read the text. The walking tour of London offers students the opportunity to interact with teachers and peers portraying characters from the text (see Chapter 1 vignette, "Using art and drama to open doors to the intellectual content of the curriculum").

Unit Four: Myths, Short Stories, and Tall Tales
 	
Students read American myths, short stories, and tall tales.
	• Students write responses to open-ended questions.
	• Introduction to:
	  * Doing research (choosing a topic, research, note taking, outlining).
	  * Writing a research report (introduction, body, conclusion, bibliography).
		• Instruction on usage as it pertains to research report writing.
		• Instruction on spelling rules.
		• Continued work on parts of speech.
			Language arts and social studies teachers collaborate on Westward Expansion research project.

Grade Six Curriculum (continued)

Literature	Writing	Language Study	Additional Information

Unit Five: The Journey of Change in the Native American Culture
 	
Students read Native American literature, including myths, legends, short stories, poetry, and nonfiction such as "Chief Seattle," "Thunder Butte," and "Medicine Bag."
	• Introduction to:
	  * Persuasive writing based on literature (includes using logic and rhetoric to support arguments).
	  * Writing poetry based on literature.
		• Vocabulary to accompany Native American literature unit.
		• Instruction on writing sentences; correcting run-on sentences and sentence fragments.	

Unit Six: Julie of the Wolves Students read *Julie of the Wolves* by Elizabeth George. Focus on: • Continued analysis of character development tied to the journey of change theme. • Analyzing perspectives in literature: compare and contrast.	• Students write responses to open-ended questions. • Review of each type of writing for the year. • Portfolio: Students choose selections to include in writing portfolios.	• Vocabulary to accompany *Julie of the Wolves*.	*Julie of the Wolves* is the story of how an Eskimo girl, lost on the tundra, is adopted by a family of wolves and saved from certain death.
Unit Seven: Endings Students read stories about Asian Americans: "The All-American Slurp" *A Jar of Dreams*	• Final portfolio entries selected and edited.	• Grammar review. • Oral presentation: "Grammar Rocks."	Students have been studying grammar throughout the year in the context of their writing and reading and in mini-lessons. The "Grammar Rocks" assignment reinforces the grammar lessons; students demonstrate their knowledge by creating and presenting songs.

A Comprehensive Curriculum for the Middle Grades

The second curriculum profile, which we have developed, draws upon teachers' knowledge and experience, research on language arts curriculum, and the *New Standards*™ *Student Performance Standards*. We used the *New Standards* because we wanted to mirror the work of the teachers we interviewed, many of whom are required to use these or similarly explicit standards documents. The *New Standards* includes specific descriptions of what students are expected to know and be able to do, as well as suggestions for projects that allow students to demonstrate that they have achieved particular standards.

Themes and Literature

In developing this curriculum for grades 6 through 8, we began by identifying themes—big ideas that students could explore through the language arts—to provide coherence and promote higher-level thinking. Many of the novels that are regularly used in the middle grades incorporate social studies subject matter, so we turned to the *Curriculum Standards for Social Studies* for our themes. We realize that districts often have their own social studies requirements at particular grades which may not parallel those on which we have chosen to focus. Our purpose in developing this curriculum profile is to provide an example of how social studies themes can be integrated into a language arts curriculum, not to make a prescription for such integration. We hope it will inspire teachers, schools, and districts to design curricula that address the components of excellence described throughout this guide, while taking into account their own particular standards and requirements.

The curriculum profile integrates the following social studies themes:

- The influence of people's assumptions, values, and beliefs on cultural understanding.
- How history helps us make informed decisions in the present.
- The nature of a just society.

Once these themes were established, the next step was to identify literature, from a variety of genres, to accompany each theme. We knew from our interviews with language arts educators that middle-grades teachers often feel obliged to use a single work of literature with their entire class, regardless of the difficulty of the text. We wanted to provide alternatives to this practice, which can lead to chapter-by-chapter "round robin reading" in classrooms where some students are unable to read the text on their own.

We chose literature titles for each theme that varied in level of difficulty. The curriculum thereby gives students opportunities to use the language arts to explore complex, theme-related ideas with texts written at an appropriate level of difficulty—an independent level if students are reading on their own, and an instructional level if they are working with the teacher. (The appendix to this profile provides a list of selected literature, categorized by theme and reading level, which illustrates the range of options teachers can draw upon.) However, some teachers must use required novels that are too difficult for some students. The curriculum incorporates a variety of strategies for working with struggling readers, including discussion, writing, using audio and video versions of texts, and flexible grouping.

Standards

We then turned to the *New Standards*. Using a curriculum mapping process, we identified those standards that would be the focus for each grade, being certain to capitalize on the connections between reading, writing, speaking, and listening. We used the examples of tasks and student work in the *New Standards* to plan projects that would allow students to demonstrate their learning. Initially, we were concerned that these examples would too severely constrain teachers' and students' creativity and choice. As it turned out, the examples were most helpful in providing us with models that encourage creativity and incorporate many opportunities for teacher and student ownership and choice.

Academic Rigor, Equity, and Developmental Appropriateness

In planning this curriculum, we wanted to create a rigorous course of study that would challenge students to reach high standards, teach them to use the language arts to explore and understand complex ideas, and provide instruction in the skills and processes that support this exploration. Further, we wanted to provide pathways to success for all students, particularly those who have struggled in traditional language arts classrooms. Our planning was guided by the assumption that all students can be successful if instruction is guided by ongoing assessment, builds on students' current knowledge, and is engaging and meaningful. We included a wide range of instructional approaches and classroom activities to meet the specific learning needs of individual students. Finally, we wanted the curriculum to be developmentally appropriate. That is, we wanted it to be based on the knowledge of how young adolescents think, suited to their age and interests, and attentive to their developing need for interactions with peers. We organized activities to help students develop from concrete to more abstract thinking and take increasing responsibility for monitoring and directing their learning, built in multiple ways for students to make connections between their lives in school and out of school, and provided many opportunities for students to collaborate and learn from each other.

Assessment

Although there is no explicit mention of assessment in the curriculum profile that follows, the assumption is that ongoing assessment will guide teaching and learning. Teachers' instructional decisions should be informed by student assessment data. As an example, in enacting this curriculm, teachers would give students rubrics (scoring guides) for their projects and writing assignments. The rubrics would articulate specific guidelines for projects and provide descriptions of the components of successful performance so that students would understand the goals for their assignments and work toward them. In addition, teachers would conduct ongoing informal and formal assessments, integrating student observations and multiple-choice, short-answer, essay, and open-ended questions within the various components of the curriculum. Teachers would make instruction and practice in test-taking skills meaningful for students by integrating them into the context of ongoing class work.

Grade Level Focus

Within the context of this comprehensive plan for grades 6 to 8, it remained to sketch out a primary focus for each year.

Grade Six: Genre study. The sixth-grade language arts curriculum focuses on genre study. This provides students with an understanding of the purposes and structures of various literary genres and builds a foundation for future reading. The yearlong theme is "The influence of people's assumptions, values, and beliefs on cultural understanding."

Throughout the year, students read theme-related novels, short stories, plays, poetry, biography, nonfiction, myths, folktales, and trickster stories. They learn about the structures of these different texts and develop reading strategies that support their comprehension. Students are expected to write narrative and descriptive passages. They memorize and write poetry. They are introduced to the research process, conduct interviews, and write research reports. They give oral presentations. In addition, during the year, students read 25 texts on their own (a requirement of the *New Standards*), maintain a log of their responses to those texts, and create an annotated bibliography of their reading. Students keep track of their independent reading on computers at school; over the three years of the curriculum, they learn to organize and sort information about their readings in a database.

Grade Seven: Studies on the theme "How history helps us make informed decisions in the present." Students begin the school year by reexamining the genres that they studied in grade 6. The selected readings extend the sixth-grade theme ("The influence of people's assumptions, values, and beliefs on cultural understanding") to include the role of social institutions and cultures in establishing values and beliefs. As the year progresses, students read historical literature such as the books *Tituba of Salem Village, The Witch of Blackbird Pond, Sign of the Beaver, April Morning, My Brother Sam Is Dead, The House of Dies Drear, Women in the Civil War,* and *To Be a Slave.* They also read more contemporary novels such as *Walk Two Moons* and *Scorpions.* They view *A Midsummer Night's Dream.* Students read, discuss, and write about the values and beliefs portrayed in the literature. They identify the sources of those values and beliefs and analyze how they contributed to or posed obstacles to cultural understanding. Students then apply their knowledge: they study and analyze current events, examining the values and beliefs that shape these events.

Grade Eight: Studies on the theme "The nature of a just society." Students in the middle grades have a strong sense of justice and what is fair. The eighth-grade curriculum allows them to consider the subtleties of these concepts (decency, integrity, morality, equality, impartiality) and to answer questions that include:

• What is a just society?
• What is fairness?

- How are justice and fairness the same?
- How are they different?

As the year unfolds, all students read the novels *Lyddie, The Giver,* and *Roll of Thunder, Hear My Cry.* Examples of activities that support struggling readers, such as listening to audiotapes, "buddy reading," journal writing, and "literature circles" are included. Students also have the opportunity to read theme-related literature based on their interests and/or reading levels. Their choices include fiction and nonfiction selections (in different media) such as *The Contender; Malcolm X: By Any Means Necessary; Another Way to Dance; Buried Onions; Rosa Parks: My Story; Drive-By; Freedom Songs; Going Where I'm Coming From: Memoirs of American Youth; West Side Story; The Gold Cadillac; Goodbye, Vietnam;* and *Hoops.*

Throughout the year, students work independently and in groups, and are encouraged to share and learn from one another's different perspectives. They do both traditional and Internet research. They listen to speakers from their community who lived through the Great Depression. They conduct interviews with local veterans of the Civil Rights Movement, the Vietnam War, and other political and cultural upheavals. The culminating project requires them to create a "Guidebook for a Just Society" in which they demonstrate their understanding of the theme.

Putting It All Together

In the tables that follow, we show a month-by-month curriculum plan for grades 6, 7, and 8. Activities are organized according to the major categories for language arts standards: reading and literature, writing, and oral language and viewing. A summary of the work for the month and some additional information appear in the left-hand column. As in the previous profile, brief definitions of terms that may be unfamiliar follow the first occurrence of each term. These terms are printed in boldface.

Comprehensive Curriculum Profile: Grade 6

Major Theme: The influence of people's assumptions, values, and beliefs on cultural understanding

September

Summary

Students are introduced to genres and the year's theme; they learn classroom routines and expectations.

Additional Information

The *New Standards* require that students read 25 full-length texts per year. The independent reading program is designed to enable students to meet this expectation.

Reading and Literature	Writing	Oral Language and Viewing
• Introduce independent reading program. Set expectations and have students begin reading and responding to their reading. • Students learn to select books that will support their reading development (books that are not too easy, not too difficult). • Students are introduced to four genres (fiction, nonfiction, poetry, and drama) and the year's theme. • Through the use of a **jigsaw** activity students compare and contrast how different genres treat similar themes. (In a jigsaw activity, students form "home teams" equal in number to the number of topics to be discussed. Each student in a home team has the task of becoming an expert on one of the topics. Expert groups, composed of students from each of the home teams, meet and study; students then return to their home teams and teach their topic to their teammates.)	• Students learn the structures and routines of the curriculum: * calendar for planning and assignments * **independent reading journals** (Students use independent reading journals to record their responses during ongoing reading.) * **annotated booklists** (Students write a one-paragraph annotation for each of their 25 independent reading books.) • Students are introduced to the writing process as they compose a reading journal entry. • Students are introduced to compare/contrast thinking through the use of a Venn diagram or similar **graphic organizer.** (Graphic organizers are diagrams that include words and pictures. Their structures indicate the relationship between the ideas displayed.) • Students are introduced to **peer editing.** (In peer editing, students work in pairs or small groups, using their knowledge of conventions and mechanics to edit each other's drafts.)	• Students learn guidelines for discussion: * Take turns. * Solicit opinions. * Respond to questions. * Give reasons to support an opinion. * Clarify or expand an idea.

Comprehensive Curriculum Profile: Grade 6 (continued)

	Reading and Literature	Writing	Oral Language and Viewing

October
 	
Summary
Students read and learn about short stories as they explore the year's theme. Students learn about the structure of narrative paragraphs and the elements of the short story; they discuss literary texts and compare and contrast texts.
	• Students begin to investigate the yearlong theme of cultural understanding, reading short stories that illuminate the theme, such as "After You, My Dear Alphonse," "Broken Chain," and "Eleven."
	• Students learn the elements of short stories:
	  * plot
	  * narrative structure
	  * character
	  * setting
	• Ongoing independent reading.
		• Narrative paragraphs: Students learn about paragraph structure and linking words.
		• Students compare and contrast the literary merits of two short stories using a graphic organizer. Students do not yet write an essay based on the organizer: the focus is on compare/contrast thinking.
		• Ongoing work on booklists and writing in reading journals: Students learn how to support an idea using references to the text.
			• Discussion groups: Students discuss theme in the short stories. Students practice the discussion guidelines, with focus on taking turns, soliciting opinions, and responding to questions.
			• Discussion groups: Students discuss the literary merits of the stories. Students practice the discussion guidelines, with focus on giving reasons that support your position.

November **Summary** Students study features of descriptive writing and learn and practice strategies for understanding texts.	• Genre study (Informational texts): Students learn form and function of informational texts structured to describe. • Literary analysis: Focus on text structure and linking words. Introduce **reciprocal teaching** strategies to aid in comprehension of text. (Reciprocal teaching is a set of comprehension-monitoring strategies. Students learn to predict, question, summarize, and clarify as they read; discussion is a critical feature.) • Ongoing independent reading.	• Students learn to summarize. • Students learn features of descriptive texts using a graphic organizer (topic and supporting details). • Ongoing work on booklists and writing in reading journals.	• Students have guided practice in reciprocal teaching discussions in small groups.

Comprehensive Curriculum Profile: Grade 6 (continued)

	Reading and Literature	Writing	Oral Language and Viewing
December **Summary** Students read, analyze, discuss, and write poetry related to the yearlong theme and make an oral presentation using the descriptive writing structure.	• Genre study (Poetry): Students learn about poetry: * What is poetry? (Focus on appeal to senses/sounds.) * How do we read poetry? * Poetic devices (rhyme, meter, simile, and metaphor). * How are themes expressed in poetry? • Ongoing independent reading.	• Ongoing practice of the writing process: * Students write a compare/contrast paragraph, discussing similarities and differences in two poems with a similar theme. How do the authors use rhyme, similes, and metaphors to explore the theme "The influence of people's assumptions, values, and beliefs on cultural understanding"? * Students write theme-related poetry. • Ongoing work on booklists and writing in reading journals.	• Students learn about **literature circles** and the roles taken by participants. (Literature circles provide structure and purpose to students' discussions of texts, giving participants particular roles to play in the discussion. Different students direct the discussion, choose interesting or difficult vocabulary, select compelling passages, and illustrate the theme. Each student can then make a unique contribution to the literature discussion.) • Students use literature circles to discuss poems. • Students memorize and recite a poem of their choice. • Oral presentation: Students give three reasons for selecting their poem, based on the descriptive graphic organizer. (Because the focus is on use of oral language skills and the structure of description, the content of the presentation is intentionally less challenging than the content of related writing activities.)

Comprehensive Curriculum Profile: Grade 6 (continued)

	Reading and Literature	Writing	Oral Language and Viewing

January
 	
Summary
Students read, respond to, and discuss theme-based novels, practice comprehension strategies, and write descriptive essays.
	• Genre study (Theme-based novels): Students learn that novels and short stories utilize the same literary elements. Based on their reading levels, students are assigned to a theme-related novel (*Journey to Jo'burg, Maniac Magee, Sounder,* or *The Cay*).
	• Students learn and practice strategies for reading with understanding:
	  * reciprocal teaching
	  * drawing inferences
	  * **Question-Answer-Response (QAR)** (QAR is a questioning strategy. Students learn to ask and answer literal and inferential questions.)
	• Ongoing independent reading of theme-based novels.
		• Students write descriptive essays with a controlling idea, relevant information, text evidence to support assertions, and a conclusion.
		• Students write in their reading journals about the novels:
		  * Personal responses.
		  * Responses to teacher prompts such as the exploration of literary elements in the novels.
		• Ongoing work on booklists and writing in reading journals.
			• Students participate in literature circles to respond to the novels.
			• Guided practice in reciprocal teaching for sections of the novels.

Comprehensive Curriculum Profile: Grade 6 (continued)

	Reading and Literature	Writing	Oral Language and Viewing
February **Summary** Students read and learn about biography; learn research skills, including conducting interviews and taking notes; and write a compare/contrast essay about the subjects of their research and their reading.	• Genre study (Biography): Students select and read a science- or technology-related biography at their independent reading level. Focus on: * What is biography? * Subjective vs. factual information in biography. * Verifying factual information with primary sources. • Students explore the question, "How have science and technology influenced, and been influenced by, individuals, societies, and cultures?" • Students read "Virginia Hamilton" by Lee Bennett Hopkins to provide them with background information about interviews (see "Writing"). • Ongoing independent reading.	• Students maintain a journal on biography, considering how the subject of their biography was influenced by, and influenced, science or technology. • Research: Students interview an individual from their community whose work is related to science or technology. * Students learn and practice note-taking skills. * Students prepare an **"I-Search"** details the student's search for information, along with the specific information gathered.) • Students write a compare/contrast essay: How is your interviewee unique? How is he/she like other people we've read about? • Ongoing work on booklists and writing in reading journals.	• In small groups, students interview a family or community member to determine how science or technology has influenced the interviewee. • Students learn interviewing and oral language skills: * Ask relevant questions. * Respond to questions with appropriate elaboration. * Use language cues to indicate different levels of hypothesizing (e.g., What if...? I'm unsure whether...). * Confirm understanding by paraphrasing.
March **Summary** Students read, view, analyze, and present a play and explore how the theme of cultural understanding emerges in drama. **Additional Information** *Brian's Song* tells the story of dying football player Brian Piccolo, depicting his relationship with fellow player Gale Sayers.	• Genre study (Drama): Students read the play *Brian's Song*. Students learn about: * how to read a play * dialogue and staging * foreshadowing * characters and themes • Students read nonfiction articles about Brian Piccolo. • Ongoing independent reading.	• Students write an essay in which they describe how the values and beliefs of the main characters in the play contribute to their friendship. • Ongoing work on booklists and writing in reading journals.	• Students practice oral presentation skills through reading and presenting sections of the play. (This will set the stage for oral presentations in May.) • Students either view a play on video or attend a performance of a play.

Comprehensive Curriculum Profile: Grade 6 (continued)

	Reading and Literature	Writing	Oral Language and Viewing

April/May
 	
Summary
Students read a variety of nonfiction selections; write a research paper that explores the yearlong theme; and learn additional oral presentation skills in preparation for a year-end project (see June, below).
	• Genre study (Nonfiction): Students read personal narratives, articles from the media and the Internet, biography, autobiography, letters, and essays for their research project (see "Writing"):
	  * Practice and apply reading strategies.
	  * Read for information.
	• Ongoing independent reading.
		• Theme-related research project: Students select a culture to research and write about. Their research paper is to report on the values and beliefs of the culture, and factors that shape and/or are shaped by values and beliefs.
		  Students learn to:
		  * Develop a controlling idea.
		  * Select an organizing structure for the report.
		  * Include appropriate facts and details.
		  * Exclude extraneous information.
		  * Write a conclusion.
		• Ongoing work on booklists and writing in reading journals.
			• Students learn additional oral presentation skills in preparation for group project in June:
			  * Know and appeal to the audience.
			  * Organize content by importance and impact.
			  * Use notes to structure the presentation.
			  * Engage the audience and maintain eye contact.

June
 	
Summary
Students study oral narratives from different cultures and work in groups to prepare and deliver a lesson about one type of narrative.
	• Genre study (Narratives from different cultures): Students read fables, trickster tales, folktales, and origin tales. They learn about literature that arose from the beliefs and values of different cultures.
	  * how to read folktales
	  * the oral tradition
	  * literature of daily life
	  * fables that teach lessons
	  * myths that explain natural phenomena
	• Ongoing independent reading.
		• Students submit final annotated booklists.
		• Ongoing writing in reading journals.
			• Students work in jigsaw groups. Each group becomes the "experts" in one of the types of stories (e.g., fables, trickster tales).
			• Each expert group prepares a lesson that they then teach to class members. The lesson incorporates the essential characteristics of the type of story the group has studied.

Comprehensive Curriculum Profile: Grade 7

Major Theme: How history helps us make informed decisions in the present

September	Reading and Literature	Writing	Oral Language and Viewing

Summary
 	
Students are reintroduced to the structures and routines of the language arts curriculum and draft a compare/contrast essay based on their theme-based reading.
	• Reintroduce independent reading program. Set expectations and have students begin reading and responding to their reading.
	• Genre review: Students read short stories, poetry, essays, and plays related to the grade 6 theme, "The influence of people's assumptions, values, and beliefs on cultural understanding."
	• Review strategies for reading different genres.
	• Students learn to make and support assertions with evidence from the texts.
		• Review requirements and format for independent reading journals and annotated booklists.
		• Review compare/contrast paragraph structure and words that signal this structure (e.g., "on the other hand").
		• Students write the first draft of a compare/contrast essay based on group-developed graphic organizers (see "Oral Language and Viewing").
		• Students revise their drafts based on feedback from peer editing groups and teacher instruction on compare/contrast structure.
			• Review guidelines for discussion: Take turns, solicit opinions, respond to questions, give reasons to support an opinion, clarify or expand an idea.
			• Practice using discussion guidelines: In groups, students create a graphic organizer to compare and contrast the benefits and weaknesses of each genre as a tool for exploring the theme.
			• Review procedures for peer editing discussions.
			• Students participate in individual conferences about their writing. They learn and practice skills for conferences including:
			  * initiating new topics
			  * asking relevant questions
			  * responding to questions

Comprehensive Curriculum Profile: Grade 7 (continued)

	Reading and Literature	Writing	Oral Language and Viewing

October/November
 	
Summary
Students begin yearlong reading of four novels related to U.S. history through the Civil War. Written and oral work on the first selection provides a bridge from the grade 6/September theme ("The influence of people's assumptions, values, and beliefs on cultural understanding") to the new theme ("How history helps us make informed decisions in the present").
 	
Additional Information
The goal is for students to use what they learn about history in social studies to make decisions in the present. Instruction in the values and beliefs of people in Puritan New England is provided in social studies. Students also use skills for group discussion learned in grade 6.
	• Students read either *Tituba of Salem Village* or *The Witch of Blackbird Pond*. (Match students with the most appropriate text based on level of difficulty.)
	• Students read nonfiction articles about Puritan New England.
	• Ongoing independent reading.
		• Review how to support an idea using references to the text.
		• Students write a response to the assigned text in which they use references to the novel and information from social studies readings to articulate and support their ideas.
		  *What were the values and beliefs prevalent among the Puritans in New England?
		  * What were the sources of those values and beliefs?
		  * How did those values and beliefs contribute or pose obstacles to cultural understanding?
		• Review the writing process.
		• Ongoing work on booklists and writing in reading journals.
			• Students participate in discussion groups based on the assigned reading, and practice discussion guidelines with focus on taking turns, soliciting opinions, and responding to questions.
			• Informal group presentations: Students identify and define a problem in the present society that is similar to those faced by characters in the novels. Students generate possible solutions to the problem, select the optimal solution, and present it to the class.

Comprehensive Curriculum Profile: Grade 7 (continued)

	Reading and Literature	Writing	Oral Language and Viewing
December **Summary** Students will resume their theme-related work after the holiday break. This month they view a contemporary version of a Shakespeare play (suggested reading in the *New Standards*), read sections of the text, and write a review of the movie version.	• After viewing *A Midsummer Night's Dream*, students read selected portions of the play that illustrate literary devices. Focus is on: 　* Drama as a literary form. 　* Literary devices, including figurative language, dialogue. 　* The language of Shakespeare. • Students read and analyze movie reviews from newspapers. • Ongoing independent reading.	• Students keep a journal in which they respond to *A Midsummer Night's Dream*. • Students write a movie review that: 　* Judges the extent to which the play is a source of entertainment. 　* Makes and supports assertions about the play with evidence from it. • Ongoing work on booklists and writing in reading journals.	• Students view a videotaped version of *A Midsummer Night's Dream*. • Students discuss sections of the play in literature circles, practicing individual roles. • Students read aloud scenes from the play.
January/February **Summary** Students focus on the theme, "How history helps us make informed decisions in the present." They hold a town meeting in which they apply their learning to discussion of a current event. Students learn the typical structure of newspaper accounts, summarize and compare newspaper accounts, and write newspaper accounts. **Additional Information** Students' study of novels about the American Revolution coincides with a social studies unit on the American Revolution.	• Students read a novel about the American Revolution. (See the list of suggested texts in the appendix.) 　* Identify recurring themes. 　* Identify the effect of point of view. 　* Analyze the reasons for a character's actions. 　* Make inferences and draw conclusions about characters, setting, and theme. 　* Identify the effects of dialogue and description. • Students read and analyze newspaper accounts and historical records of an event that occurred during the American Revolution, and newspaper accounts of a current event. 　* Read critically. 　* Identify the author's purpose and stance. 　* Analyze the positions advanced and the evidence offered in support of them. • Ongoing independent reading.	• Students write summaries of selected newspaper accounts and historical records. • Students write a news account of an event from the American Revolution. • Students write a report that compares and contrasts newspaper accounts and historical records of a single event. Students explain the reasons for similarities and differences in the treatment of the same event. • Students write a report that compares and contrasts the treatment of a current event by different newspapers. Students explain possible reasons for similarities and differences in the treatment of the same event. • Ongoing work on booklists and writing in reading journals.	• Students work in groups organized by level of difficulty of texts read or by common interests. • Students discuss the theme, character, setting, dialogue, and description of the novels they are reading in literature circles. • Students hold a town meeting in which they take a stance about a current event, illustrating their understanding of the theme. Using fiction and nonfiction sources, they: 　* Display turn-taking behaviors. 　* Offer their own opinions without dominating. 　* Actively solicit others' comments and opinions. 　* Respond appropriately. 　* Give reasons to support their opinions. 　* Clarify or expand a response. 　* Employ a group decision-making process.

Comprehensive Curriculum Profile: Grade 7 (continued)

	Reading and Literature	Writing	Oral Language and Viewing

March/April/May
 	
Summary
Students read fiction and nonfiction texts focusing on the Civil War, learn research skills, and write and present their research orally and on the web. Students' reading is guided by the question, "What am I learning from history that I can use in my own life?"
 	
Additional Information
Cobblestone and *Footsteps* are middle-grades journals that focus on American and African American history.
	• Students read:
	  * A Civil War novel.
	  * A nonfiction selection about the Civil War.
	  * Articles that pertain to the Civil War from *Cobblestone* and *Footsteps*.
	  * Informational texts from their social studies classroom.
	  * Internet and library articles and books.
	• Independent and **buddy reading.** (In buddy reading, strong readers are paired with less able readers.)
	• Ongoing independent reading (of Civil War literature).
		• Students learn research skills:
		  * Use the Internet and library.
		  * Analyze the quality of the information.
		  * Decide the level of analysis (breadth vs. depth).
		  * Take notes.
		  * Summarize.
		• Students write a report in which they describe the lessons they have learned from their study of the Civil War and how they might use that information in their own lives.
		  Students learn to:
		  * Engage the reader by establishing a context.
		  * Develop a controlling idea that conveys a perspective on the subject.
		  * Create an organizing structure appropriate to purpose, audience, and context.
		  * Include appropriate facts and details.
		  * Exclude extraneous and inappropriate information.
		• Ongoing work on booklists and writing in reading journals.
			• Students discuss the novels in literature circles.
			• Students work in small groups composed of students with a range of reading levels to share research information.
			• Students write final reports independently.
			• Students prepare and deliver individual presentations on the lessons they have learned from their study of the Civil War and how they might use that information in their own lives.
			  Students learn to:
			  * Shape the information to appeal to the interests of the audience.
			  * Shape the content and organization according to importance and impact (not the availability of information).
			  * Use notes and memory aids to structure the presentation.
			  * Develop several main points relating to a single thesis.
			  * Project their personality in selecting, organizing, and delivering content.
			• Groups work together to create a web-based project that extends their research to the present.

Comprehensive Curriculum Profile: Grade 7 (continued)

	Reading and Literature	Writing	Oral Language and Viewing

June
 	
Summary
The year ends by moving from a historical focus to contemporary issues. Students work in groups to read and analyze a contemporary novel, focusing on the impact of literary elements. They write and present a skit that demonstrates their understanding by using literary devices to portray a character from the novel.
 	
Additional Information
Given the potential range of reading levels, audiotapes (available for the suggested novels) should be used to provide all students access to the text, regardless of their reading levels. This is appropriate because the focus of the activity is on teaching students about literature, not on teaching reading skills and strategies (which would require students to work with texts consistent with their instructional reading levels).
	• Groups of students read the same contemporary novel (e.g., *Walk Two Moons, The Outsiders*). Students:
	  * Identify the impact of the author's decisions regarding word choice, content, and use of literary elements.
	  * Evaluate literary merit.
	  * Identify the effect of point of view.
	  * Analyze the reasons for a character's actions.
	  * Identify the effect of literary devices, particularly dialogue.
	• Ongoing independent reading.
		• Students submit their final annotated booklists.
		• Students work in groups to write a skit that is based on an incident in the novel and that illustrates the theme ("How history helps us make informed decisions about the present").
		• Ongoing writing in reading journals.
			• Students discuss their reading in literature circles.
			• Students present their skits to the class.

Comprehensive Curriculum Profile: Grade 8

Major Theme: The nature of a just society

September/October	Reading and Literature	Writing	Oral Language and Viewing

Summary
Students are reintroduced to the structures and routines of the language arts curriculum, and are introduced to the major theme for the year, "The nature of a just society."
 	
Additional Information
Students in the middle grades have a strong sense of justice and what is "fair." The yearlong focus on the theme of a just society will allow them to consider the subtleties of concepts such as decency, integrity, morality, equality, and impartiality.
	• Introduce yearlong, theme-related newspaper project. Each month students will read teacher-selected newspaper articles about a theme-related topic from different newspapers; they will use the Internet to access articles from different states and countries.
	• Students compare and contrast the treatment of a similar topic by different newspapers.
	• Students read theme-related selections from informational text, short stories, poetry, and drama. (Selections are available in text and audiotape versions in published literature anthologies; see Chapter 4 for information.)
	   * Review literary devices of each genre.
	   * Make assertions about the texts and support with evidence.
	   * Evaluate the writing strategies and elements of the author's craft.
	   * Compare/contrast the treatment of the theme by each of the genres. What are the merits of each?
	• Ongoing independent reading.
		• Students begin grade 8 annotated booklists and learn the computer skills to create a database to organize their lists.
		• Students select one of the assigned newspaper articles.
		   * Summarize the article.
		   * Discuss the article in relation to the idea of a just society (see "Oral Language").
		   * Write about the relevance of the article to an issue of fairness or justice in their own communities.
		• Introduce yearlong group writing project which will culminate in the creation of a guidebook for a just society reflecting students' yearlong study of various genres.
		• Begin independent reading journals; responses will relate to the theme of the just society.
		• Students select a theme-related short story, poem, play, and nonfiction text and write a paper in which they compare and contrast how each genre treats the theme.
			• Students use discussion of the assigned newspaper articles to explore the idea of a just society. They follow discussion guidelines: take turns, solicit opinions, respond to questions, give reasons to support an opinion, clarify or expand an idea.
			• Review procedures for peer editing discussions.
			• Students participate in literature circles and informal discussions of various texts/genres.

Comprehensive Curriculum Profile: Grade 8 (continued)

November/December	Reading and Literature	Writing	Oral Language and Viewing
Summary Students read and analyze a novel, using as a lens the theme of a just society. They write narrative diary entries, participate in group discussions, and conduct research about the historical period in which the novel is set.	• Students read *Lyddie*. • Students conduct research related to the social and political contexts of the Industrial Revolution, using the Internet and the library. • Ongoing independent reading.	• Students write narrative diary entries describing the injustices faced by workers in the Lowell mills. Their entries: * Engage the reader. * Establish the characters, setting, plot, and conflict. * Have an organizing structure. * Use appropriate details and language to develop the plot and characters. • Students write an I-Search essay documenting their research about the Industrial Revolution. • Ongoing work on booklists and writing in reading journals.	• In their discussion groups, students: * Read diary entries aloud. * Engage in peer editing. * Discuss the social conditions that allowed the injustices in *Lyddie* to occur, the societal changes that could have prevented these injustices, and the societal changes that actually occurred in response to these injustices.

Comprehensive Curriculum Profile: Grade 8 (continued)

	Reading and Literature	Writing	Oral Language and Viewing

January/February
 	
Summary
Students read and analyze a second theme-related novel. They compare text and video versions, interview community members about the historical era in which the novel is set, and make oral presentations based on their interview data.
 	
Additional Information
Roll of Thunder, Hear My Cry is written at the eighth-grade level. The complex issues it addresses increase its difficulty. Prereading activities will build students' background knowledge about the Depression era, particularly as it affected sharecroppers in the South (e.g., brainstorming discussions to elicit knowledge about the Depression and sharecroppers, videos, or additional reading about this historical period). In addition, viewing the video of *Roll of Thunder, Hear My Cry* and having audiotape versions available make the novel more accessible to struggling readers and set the stage for exploration of the theme.
	• Students read *Roll of Thunder, Hear My Cry* and focus on:
	  * Author's choice of words and content.
	  * Use of dialogue.
	  * Characterization.
	  * Point of view.
	  * Plot.
	  * Making inferences.
	  * Ongoing exploration of the theme "The nature of a just society."
	• Ongoing independent reading.
		• Students write an essay in which they examine the causes and effects of an incident that appears in both the video and text of *Roll of Thunder*.
		  * Students use a cause and effect graphic organizer.
		  * Writing process focus is on revision.
		• Review note-taking skills:
		  * for interviews
		  * for guidebook
		• Ongoing work on booklists and writing in reading journals.
			• Students view a video of *Roll of Thunder* prior to reading the novel.
			• Students read selected passages orally and analyze and discuss them.
			• One-on-one writing conferences with the teacher.
			• Peer editing discussions.
			• Community members who lived through the Depression speak to students.
			  * Students prepare questions to ask speakers.
			  * Students ask relevant questions and use note-taking strategies to record responses.
			• Students make small group presentations of interview data in which they demonstrate the ability to:
			  * Shape and organize content.
			  * Develop several main points relating to a single thesis.
			  * Engage the audience.

Comprehensive Curriculum Profile: Grade 8 (continued)

March/April

Summary

Students read and analyze Holocaust literature and view a video of a speech by Hitler. They learn about propaganda techniques and develop techniques for writing a persuasive essay in the form of an editorial.

Reading and Literature	Writing	Oral Language and Viewing

• Students read theme-related Holocaust fiction and nonfiction. They learn strategies for critical reading and have opportunities for guided practice in instructional-level texts.
• Students read public documents (documents that focus on public policy at the national, state, or local level) along with Internet and conventional research sources related to the Holocaust and World War II.
• Students learn strategies for understanding complex texts:
  * Summarizing.
  * Note taking.
  * Identifying author's purpose and stance.
  * Analyzing arguments.
  * Propaganda techniques.
• Ongoing independent reading.
	• Students write persuasive essays (editorials) in response to the public address (see "Oral Language"), public documents, and conventional research (see "Reading"). They learn to:
	  * Use reasoned arguments to support an opinion.
	  * Develop a controlling idea that represents a clear and knowledge-able viewpoint.
	  * Use a structure that is appropriate to the needs, values, and interests of a specific audience.
	  * Arrange details effectively and persuasively.
	  * Anticipate and address reader concerns and counter-arguments.
	  * Support arguments with detailed evidence, citing sources as appropriate.
	  * Write a conclusion.
	• Ongoing work on booklists and writing in reading journals.
		• Students hold book talks to discuss the fiction and nonfiction texts. Because students are reading many different titles, the content of the book talks is open-ended. Students follow discussion guidelines.
		• Students view videos of a public address by Hitler and identify propaganda techniques in the address.
		• Students participate in group discussions of the theme in relation to the readings and video.
		• One-on-one writing conferences with the teacher.
		• Peer editing conferences.

Comprehensive Curriculum Profile: Grade 8 (continued)

Reading and Literature	Writing	Oral Language and Viewing
May/June **Summary** Students draw on the year's work to help them identify the characteristics of a just society. They write a guidebook, in the form of public and functional documents, that articulates their vision. **Additional Information** *The Giver* (available on audiotape) addresses complex moral and social issues that are closely tied to the theme "The nature of a just society."	• Students read the contemporary novel *The Giver*. Analysis of the novel focuses on the society portrayed in the novel: What are the rules of the society? Are they fair? Are they just? Whom do they benefit? Who suffers? Who decides the rules? Who enforces the rules? How? How do the rules established by the elders compare with the rules of our society? How can we use the knowledge we gain from *The Giver* in creating our guidebook? • Students read and analyze functional documents (e.g., tax forms, census forms, voter registration forms) and learn to: * Identify the social context of the documents. * Identify the author's purpose and stance. * Examine the appeal of a document to friendly and hostile audiences. • Independent reading: Students read a selection of theme-related literature set in the last half of the 20th century.	• Group project: Students create a "Guide to a Just Society" which may be produced as text or as a website. It is composed of public documents articulating the policies that guide a just society (e.g., laws, a constitution, a bill of rights and responsibilities) and functional documents necessary for the operation of the society. Students: * Demonstrate an understanding of the contents and organization of public documents. * Demonstrate familiarity with a variety of functional documents. * Include information that is consistent with the audience (other students) and purpose. * Use computer formatting to make the guidebook user friendly. • Students complete their annotated booklists sortable by title, theme, genre, level of interest, etc. • Ongoing writing in reading journals.	• Students participate in literature circle discussions of *The Giver*. • Students hold book talks in which they discuss what they are learning about the theme from their independent reading. • Students work in groups on the guidebook. • Students work in groups to devise theme-related interview questions to elicit information needed for their guides. • Students interview people who have dealt with issues of justice and fairness (e.g., participants in the Civil Rights Movement, Vietnam veterans, draft resisters, women's rights activists, Japanese World War II internees). The teacher can help students locate people in the community to interview. • Each student prepares and delivers an oral presentation that reflects on the theme through the experience of the interviewee.

Appendix

Literature for Grades 6–8[3]

Themes	Literature to Accompany Themes
The influence of people's assumptions, values, and beliefs on cultural understanding	• Gardiner, *Stone Fox* (4) • Spinelli, *Wringer* (4) • George, *Julie* (5) • George, *Julie of the Wolves* (5) • George, *Julie's Wolf Pack* (5) • Myers, *Malcolm X: By Any Means Necessary* (5) • Myers, *Scorpions* (5) • O'Dell, *Sing Down the Moon* (5) • Petry, *Tituba of Salem Village* (5) • Soto, *Jesse* (5) • Spinelli, *Maniac Magee* (5) • Creech, *Walk Two Moons* (6) • Hentoff, *The Day They Came to Arrest the Book* (6) • Hinton, *Tex* (6) • Speare, *The Witch of Blackbird Pond* (6) • Taylor, *Timothy of the Cay* (6) • Twain, *The Adventures of Huckleberry Finn* (6) • Ho, *The Clay Marble* (6) • Armstrong, *Sounder* (7) • Borland, *When the Legends Die* (7) • Hinton, *The Outsiders* (7) • Hinton, *That Was Then, This Is Now* (7) • Lasky, *Beyond the Burning Time* (7) • Naidoo, *Journey to Jo'burg* (7) • Paulsen, *The Crossing* (7)	• Peck, *A Day No Pigs Would Die* (7) • Rinaldi, *In My Father's House* (7) • Taylor, *The Cay* (7) • Taylor, *Let the Circle Be Unbroken* (7) • Cormier, *The Chocolate War* (8) • Davis, *Escape to Freedom* (8) (Drama) • Lipsyte, *The Contender* (8) • Taylor, *The Road to Memphis* (8) • Taylor, *Roll of Thunder, Hear My Cry* (8) • Carnes, *Us and Them: A History of Intolerance in America* (8) • Lee, *To Kill a Mockingbird* (10) • Chavez, "The Flying Tortilla Man"* • Chippewa Traditional, "A Song of Greatness"* • Frost, *You Come Too: Poems for Young Readers* • Hughes, *The Dream Keeper and Other Poems by Langston Hughes* • Hughes, "Mother to Son"* • Hughes, "Thank You, M'am"** • Patterson, "Martin Luther King"** • Quindlen, "Homeless"** • Soto, "Seventh Grade"** • Carlson (ed.), *Cool Salsa: Bilingual Poems on Growing Up Latino in the United States*

[3] This list includes examples of literature linked to the major themes of the grades 6–8 curriculum profile. For most works, reading grade levels are indicated in parentheses.

Prentice Hall Literature: Bronze (Upper Saddle River, NJ: Prentice-Hall, 1996).

**The Language of Literature*, Grade 7 (Evanston, IL: McDougal Littell, 2000).

Appendix (continued)

Themes	Literature to Accompany Themes
Genre Study: Fantasy	• Juster, *The Phantom Tollbooth* (5) • Babbitt, *Tuck Everlasting* (6) • Hunter, *A Stranger Came Ashore* (6)	• L'Engle, *A Wrinkle in Time* (6) • O'Brien, *Z for Zachariah* (6) • Tolkien, *The Hobbit* (8)
Genre Study: Fables	• Aesop, "The Fox and the Crow" (2)* • Aesop, "The Town Mouse and the Country Mouse" *	• Ryder, "The Mice That Set Elephants Free"**
Genre Study: Tricksters and Rascals	• Courlander, "All Stories Are Anansi's"** • Malotki, "Coyote and Little Turtle"** • Bushnaq, "Djuha Borrows a Pot"	• Edmonds, "Senor Coyote and the Tricked Trickster"****
Genre Study: Folk Tales and Origin Tales	• Bruchac, *The First Strawberries: A Cherokee Story* (3) • Blair, *Tall Tale America* (6) • Robinson and Hill, "How Coyote Stole Fire" (Crow Indian)**	• Quiroga, "How the Flamingoes Got Their Stockings" (Uruguay)*** • Vo-Dinh, "The Little Lizard's Sorrow" (Vietnam)* • Kendall and Li, "The Pointing Finger" (China)*
Genre Study: Myths	• Colum, *The Golden Fleece and the Heroes Who Lived Before Achilles* (5) • D'Aulaire, *Norse Gods and Giants* • Lee, *Toad Is the Uncle of Heaven* (Vietnam)	• Serrailler, *Beowulf the Warrior* • Evslin, *The Greek Gods* • Evslin, *Heroes and Monsters of Greek Myth* • Evslin, *Trojan War*
Genre Study: Short Stories	• Twain, *The Celebrated Jumping Frog of Calaveras County* (6)	• Singer (ed.), *Stay True: Short Stories for Strong Girls* • Saki, *Surprising Stories by Saki*
Genre Study: Drama	• Blinn, *Brian's Song* (6) • Gibson, *The Miracle Worker* (7)	• Shakespeare, *A Midsummer Night's Dream* (9) • Shakespeare, *Romeo and Juliet* (9)
Genre Study: Poetry	• *Poetry USA* (journal) • Poe, *The Raven and Other Poems*	• *Reflections on a Gift of Watermelon Pickle ... and Other Modern Verse* (anthology, Scott Foresman)

*Prentice Hall Literature: Bronze (Upper Saddle River, NJ: Prentice-Hall, 1996).
***Prentice Hall Literature: Copper (Upper Saddle River, NJ: Prentice-Hall, 1996).

Appendix (continued)

Themes	Literature to Accompany Themes
How history helps us make informed decisions in the present	• Petry, *Harriet Tubman: Conductor on the Underground Railroad* (4) • Speare, *The Sign of the Beaver* (4) • Hesse, *Out of the Dust* (5) • Hunt, *Across Five Aprils* (5) • Lowry, *Number the Stars* (5) • Paulsen, *The Car* (Vietnam) (5) • Petry, *Tituba of Salem Village* (5) • Reit, *Behind Rebel Lines: The Incredible Story of Emma Edmonds, Civil War Spy* (5) • Soto, *Jesse* (Vietnam) (5–6) • Avi, *The Fighting Ground* (6) • Choi, *The Year of the Impossible Goodbyes* (6) • Collier, *My Brother Sam Is Dead* (6) • Curtis, *The Watsons Go to Birmingham—1963* (6) • Forbes, *Johnny Tremain* (6) • Hamilton, *The House of Dies Drear* (6) • Speare, *The Witch of Blackbird Pond* (6) • Yates, *Amos Fortune, Free Man* (6) • Rostkowski, *After the Dancing Days* (6) • Cushman, *Catherine, Called Birdy* (6) • Paterson, *Lyddie* (6) • Filipovic, *Zlata's Diary: A Child's Life in Sarajevo* (6) • Boas, *We Are Witnesses: Five Diaries of Teenagers Who Died in the Holocaust* (7)	• Fast, *April Morning* (7) • Hamilton, *Anthony Burns: The Defeat and Triumph of a Fugitive Slave* (7) • Keith, *Rifles for Watie* (7) • Murphy, *The Boys' War* (7) • Myers, *Fallen Angels* (7) • Wiesel, *Night* (7) • Matas, *After the War* (7) • Crane, *The Red Badge of Courage* (8) • Frank, *The Diary of a Young Girl* (8) • Haskins, *Get on Board: The Story of the Underground Railroad* (8) • Lester, *To Be a Slave* (8) • Taylor, *Roll of Thunder, Hear My Cry* (8) • Miller, *Buffalo Gals: Women of the Old West* (9) • Gies, *Anne Frank Remembered* • Isaacman, *Clara's Story* • Houston, *Farewell to Manzanar* • Wormser, *Growing Up in the Great Depression* • Weisman (ed.), *The Lowell Mill Girls* • Collier, *The Winter Hero* (mature) • Emert, *Women in the Civil War* • *Calliope* (journal/world history) • *Cobblestone* (journal/American history) • *Footsteps* (journal/African American history)
The nature of a just society	• Lowry, *Number the Stars* (5) • Greene, *Summer of My German Soldier* (6) • Pascal, *Taking Sides* (6) • Paterson, *Lyddie* (6) • Berck, *No Place to Be: Voices of Homeless Children* (7) • Galarza, *Barrio Boy* (7) • Lowry, *The Giver* (7)	• Wiesel, *Night* (7) • Frank, *The Diary of a Young Girl* (8) • Taylor, *Roll of Thunder, Hear My Cry* (8) • White, *Ryan White: My Own Story* (8) • Houston, *Farewell to Manzanar* • Weisman (ed.), *The Lowell Mill Girls*

CHAPTER 3

Annotated Resources

This chapter describes a variety of resources that language arts teachers can use to help them plan and implement standards-based curricula. It has the following nine sections:

- *Standards and Frameworks* describes major national standards documents and identifies a source of information about both national and state standards.

- *Professional Organizations* identifies national organizations that provide information about the theory and practice of language arts teaching, publish books and periodicals, and organize conferences and other professional development opportunities for educators.

- *Websites* provides examples of Internet-based sources of information about research and practice in middle-grades language arts education. These websites link to other relevant resources.

- *Curriculum Materials with Accompanying Professional Development* describes examples of curriculum programs that provide teachers with opportunities to develop teaching approaches that support student achievement of standards.

- *Professional Development Resources* describes sources of professional development programs and information.

- *Published Literature Programs and Anthologies* highlights published curriculum materials that can serve either as the core of an integrated language arts program or as a resource for teachers and students.

- *Student Reference* gives an example of a useful student reference handbook.

- *Management Tools* identifies software-based programs that help teachers determine students' reading levels and direct them to appropriate books for independent and instructional reading.

- *Professional Materials* describes a variety of examples of books that provide both theoretical and practical guidance about language arts curriculum, teaching, and learning.

Standards and Frameworks

Many of these resources were recommended by the teachers interviewed for this guide. Others were suggested by members of the advisory board or are widely recognized sources of information and wisdom about language arts curriculum and teaching. They can inform and guide the development and implementation of language arts curricula that meet the criteria of academic rigor, equity, and developmental appropriateness described in this guide.

Standards for the English Language Arts (Urbana, IL, and Newark, DE: National Council of Teachers of English and International Reading Association, 1996)

These standards were developed by NCTE and IRA, the two major professional organizations in English and language arts education (described below, under "Professional Organizations"). The document is the result of a four-year effort that involved thousands of educators, researchers, parents, policymakers, and others around the U.S. The goal of the authors of the standards document was "to define, as clearly and specifically as possible, the current consensus among literacy teachers and researchers about what students should learn in the English language arts—reading, writing, listening, speaking, viewing, and visually representing." The standards were also intended "to ensure that *all* students are offered the opportunities, the encouragement, and the vision to develop the language skills they need to pursue life's goals, including personal enrichment and participation as informed members of our society."

The first part of the document describes the need for standards, discusses the perspectives on literacy and learning that inform the standards, and lists and briefly explains the twelve standards. The rest of the document offers a series of vignettes drawn from the elementary, middle school, and high school levels that are intended to illustrate what the standards look like when applied in the classroom. Also included is a glossary and lists of the various individuals and organizations that contributed to development of the document.

These standards provide a useful framework which states and districts can use to develop more explicit standards that are consistent with the needs of their student populations. The document can be ordered from NCTE or IRA; contact information is listed below, under "Professional Organizations." Also available from NCTE are the *Standards in Practice* and *Standards Consensus* series; see below, under "Professional Materials."

New Standards™ Student Performance Standards (Washington, DC: National Center on Education and the Economy and University of Pittsburgh, 1997)

The *New Standards* are designed to make national standards in the content areas operational by not only describing what students should know and be able to do but also including numerous examples of student work illustrating what meeting the standards looks like. Each example of student work is accompanied by an explanation of how the example illustrates the relevant standard. The *New Standards* volume for the middle grades includes standards in English language arts, mathematics, science, and applied learning. In each subject area, the *New Standards* performance standards build on the content standards developed by the national professional organizations. In language arts, therefore, the *New Standards* are consistent with the NCTE/IRA standards document described above. Also accompanying each grade-level volume is a video illustrating student work for the "speaking and listening" standard. The developers of the *New Standards* have also developed a performance assessment system linked to the standards and adopted by a number of states and districts.

Available from:
National Center on Education and the Economy
P.O. Box 10391
Rochester, NY 14610
Phone: (888) 882-9538 (Customer Service)
Website: http://www.ncee.org

Council of Chief State School Officers (CCSSO)

CCSSO maintains a website with a link to each state's department of education where you can find the state standards for language arts as well as links to local district information. In collaboration with four other state-based organizations, CCSSO has also developed the State Education Improvement Partnership (SEIP), which offers a variety of activities and services to states. Among these are training in benchmarking of standards and evaluative feedback regarding states' efforts to implement standards. Information about SEIP can be found on the CCSSO website.

For information, contact
Council of Chief State School Officers
One Massachusetts Avenue NW, Suite 700
Washington, DC 20001-1431
Phone: (202) 408-5505
Website: http://www.ccsso.org

National Council of Teachers of English (NCTE)
1111 W. Kenyon Road
Urbana, IL 61801-1096
Phone: (800) 369-6283
Website: http://www.ncte.org
The National Council of Teachers of English (NCTE) is a membership organization for teachers of English and language arts at all educational levels. NCTE has about 80,000 members and sponsors 120 regional, state, and local affiliates. NCTE publishes books about the theory and

Professional Organizations

practice of English and language arts education and also produces a number of journals and other publications. Those of particular interest to middle-grades educators include *Voices from the Middle,* which specifically focuses on middle-grades concerns, and *English Journal,* which examines how theory plays out in classroom practice. NCTE holds four national conventions and conferences annually offering teachers opportunities to learn about new ideas and practices, meet colleagues from around the country, and examine materials on display by publishers. NCTE also sponsors workshops and regional and local conferences, and supports electronic communication among English language arts educators through its website and mailing list (NCTE-talk).

International Reading Association (IRA)
800 Barksdale Road
P. O. Box 8139
Newark, DE 19714-8139
Phone: (302) 731-1600
Website: http://www.reading.org
IRA is a membership organization that works to improve the quality of reading instruction through research on the teaching and learning of reading, dissemination of reading research, and public advocacy. IRA has about 90,000 members and 1250 councils and 42 national affiliates. IRA holds an annual convention and biennial world congresses as well as a number of regional conferences, and it sponsors research seminars and institutes. The association also publishes books, videotapes, and electronic products, as well as five journals. Its *Journal of Adolescent & Adult Literacy* is directed at middle school, secondary, college, and adult educators. *Reading Online* is an electronic journal for literacy educators at all levels. *Reading Research Quarterly* reports on reading theory and research. IRA's website includes "The Literacy Connection" which maintains links to a variety of resources on reading and reading instruction.

National Middle School Association (NMSA)
4151 Executive Parkway, Suite 300
Westerville, OH 43081
Phone: (800) 528-6672
Website: http://www.nmsa.org
The National Middle School Association (NMSA) serves as a voice for professionals, parents, and others interested in the educational and developmental needs of young adolescents (10–15 years of age). NMSA has over 20,000 members in more than 50 countries, including teachers, principals, parents, college faculty, central office administrators, educational consultants, and community leaders. In addition, NMSA has state, provincial, and international affiliates that work to provide middle-grades support. NMSA also has working committees and task forces that focus on specific areas: curriculum, professional preparation, publications, research, rural and small schools, and urban issues.

National Staff Development Council (NSDC)
P.O. Box 240
Oxford, OH 45056
Phone: (513) 523-6029
Website: http://www.nsdc.org/
The National Staff Development Council (NSDC) is a non-profit association committed to ensuring success for all students through staff development and school improvement. The council believes that high-quality staff development programs are key to improving learning in schools. It offers a number of publications and also sponsors projects, consultation services, leadership councils, and training for staff developers. The website offers resources and links that middle-grades educators will find helpful for planning professional development.

Center on English Learning & Achievement (CELA)
Website: http://cela.albany.edu
CELA, a national research center funded primarily by the U.S. Department of Education's Office of Educational Research and Improvement (OERI), is dedicated to improving the teaching and learning of English and language arts. CELA's research seeks to discover what elements of curriculum, instruction, and assessment are essential to developing "high literacy" and how schools can best help students achieve success. CELA defines high literacy as "the ability to use language, content, thinking, and conversation to make sense of, extend meanings about, and communicate to others concerning one's knowledge and experience." The center provides information about what works, for whom, and under what conditions to teachers, schools, and communities so that they can choose the approaches that will work with their students. CELA's research is also designed to examine the tradeoffs (including costs) involved in using different approaches to English achievement. CELA's website includes information about its current research, a newsletter, access to research reports and other publications, a discussion board, dates of upcoming presentations by its staff, and links to related resources.

MiddleWeb: Exploring Middle School Reform
Website: http://www.middleweb.com/
MiddleWeb describes itself as a website devoted to "exploring the challenges of middle school reform." Sponsored by the Edna McConnell Clark Foundation, *MiddleWeb* offers extensive resources and information of interest to any educator or parent of middle-grades students. It includes teacher and principal diaries, teacher interviews, and news items (updated weekly) which link to articles in *Education Week* and newspapers around the country. An index allows the visitor to view journal articles in categories such as Assessment and Evaluation, Curriculum and Instruction, Standards-Based School Reform, Teacher Professional

Websites

Development, and Student and School Life. There is a search option to find information within the site and links to other educational sites. A wealth of information on middle schools and school reform is accessible at this site. As of the fall of 2000, MiddleWeb is also launching a list-serve for middle-grades teachers who are "restless to improve." List members include exemplary teachers in districts across the U.S., and the list features regular guests, including experts in curriculum, professional growth, and standards-based teaching, who converse with list members. The *Guiding Curriculum Decisions* series can be downloaded from this site.

Curriculum Materials with Accompanying Professional Development

As described in Chapter 1, ongoing professional development is crucial for successful implementation of a standards-based language arts curriculum. The National Staff Development Council's *What Works in the Middle: Results-Based Staff Development*, described in the next section ("Professional Development Resources"), identifies several programs combining curriculum materials with professional development support which have been shown by research to be effective in improving student achievement. Among the teachers interviewed for this guide were a number who have used some of these materials and participated in the professional development experiences. Several of these teachers' comments about the programs are included in this section.

Junior Great Books
Great Books Foundation
35 Wacker Drive
Chicago, IL 60601-2298
Phone: (800) 222-5870
Website: http://www.greatbooks.org
Grade Levels: K–12
Research shows that the *Junior Great Books* program, in existence since 1962, "improves students' critical reading, literary analysis, and critical thinking processes as a result of engaging in shared inquiry."[1] The *Junior Great Books* "Shared Inquiry" method of reading and discussion focuses on asking interpretive questions, the fundamental questions about the meaning of a work that have no single correct answer. Students become engaged in the text through the exploration of problems and issues raised in the literature. Writing, from note taking to essays, is an integral part of students' engagement with and response to the literature.

---

[1] Joellen Killion, *What Works in the Middle: Results-Based Staff Development* (Oxford, OH: National Staff Development Council, 1999).

Materials for grades 7 through 9 include a student anthology with 12 reading selections, including short stories and novellas, and a leader's guide which includes prereading questions, interpretive questions for discussion, note-taking activities, suggested passages for textual analysis, and post-discussion writing activities. For grade 6, two anthologies are available, each of which contains 12 reading selections. There are also student activity books for grade 6. Reading selections are intentionally limited in length to allow students to reread the text and work with it closely for several days.

Implementing the *Junior Great Books* program requires that all participating staff attend a two-day Basic Leader Training Course provided by the Great Books Foundation. The training focuses on questioning and listening strategies that teachers can use to keep students engaged and focused during discussions, and on techniques for meeting the needs of students of different achievement levels. Follow-up support and advanced training are also available.

A young teacher who is just starting to use *Junior Great Books* with his sixth graders observed, "The kids enjoy it. The stories are challenging. The kids have to delve into the story and figure out what the author is trying to convey. I was surprised by some kids who usually aren't very talkative. They come out with powerful ideas. They build off what each other says, give each other ideas. They learn that they can't just give an answer and not really back it up. They learn to go back into the text. But for me it's difficult because I'm thinking something and I see that the kids are almost there and I want to kind of push them that way, but I can't. That's what I learned in the workshop. You have to let them get it on their own. And they do because they help one another out. Someone will say something and it will shoot off an idea in another person's head and they will throw it out to the group."

Reading for Real
Developmental Studies Center
2000 Embarcadero, Suite 305
Oakland, CA 94606-5300
Phone: (510) 533-0213
Website: http://www.devstu.org
Grade Levels: 4–8
Reading for Real offers complete, age-appropriate, multicultural books along with individual teaching guides for each book. A separate program manual for all grade levels suggests ways to implement the program, facilitate discussions and activities, ask provocative questions, and provide useful feedback to students. The selected books include classic and contemporary novels, biographies and autobiographies, historical narratives, short stories, and poetry. For each grade level, the series includes teacher's guides for 18 to 23 books, including one nonfiction

book. Titles of some of the seventh-grade books include *Roll of Thunder, Hear My Cry; Aliens in the Family; The Endless Steppe; I Am an American;* and *The Giver.* Students are assured access to each text, as half of the books are read aloud by the teacher and the other half are intended to be read in collaboration with student partners.

Reading for Real's structure and the professional development provided by the Developmental Studies Center help teachers learn to facilitate substantive and engaging book discussions in which students listen to each other and have the opportunity to express their ideas. This program is designed to encourage students to explore in depth themes and issues presented in the literature. Through oral language, reading, and writing, students share and further develop their thinking.

> One teacher who uses *Reading for Real* reported, "I know there is reading going on. I know there is discussion going on because the prompts in the books' 'partner pages' are so good that kids have to stop and talk, and they have to fill in a chart or express their own opinion. The kids really delve into what's going on and try to figure out why things are happening. So they're a lot more involved, and I'm not lecturing at them. This program really changed the way I teach."

Touchstones for Middle Schools
The Touchstones Discussion Project
48 West Street, Suite 104
Annapolis, MD 21401
Phone: (410) 263-2121
Website: http://www.touchstones.org/
Grade Levels: 6–8

Three senior faculty members of St. John's College in Annapolis, Maryland, developed *Touchstones,* a program designed to teach students the art of discussion with their peers. The program aims to teach students "to work cooperatively, to listen with respect and accuracy, to base decisions on available evidence, to teach themselves, to help others learn, and to devise problem-solving strategies." Over 250,000 students, ranging from elementary school students to senior citizens, have participated in *Touchstones* discussions.

The program requires one class period per week in which students sit in a circle with a teacher leader and discuss a brief, non-contemporary, multicultural text which might be anything from a Hopi Indian tale to an excerpt from Plato's *Symposium.* Each of the three middle-grades volumes contains 30 multicultural classics, each of which is a tool to connect academic topics to students' experiences. All students have access to the text because the leader reads it aloud. The students respond to a handout that initially encourages them to make connections between the text and their own experience. They then meet in small groups to compare their responses. Finally, they return to the whole group to discuss their opinions and suggestions. The texts are intended to "display the ideas of one thoughtful human being to which students compare their own." The program's developers note that if the text is given too much prominence in the beginning, the higher-performing students will dominate the class and hinder the development of effective discussion groups. Once the discussion format has been established and all students' contributions are validated, the group is able to focus more directly on analyzing and interpreting the texts. Experience has shown this program to be an effective way to encourage students of diverse backgrounds to talk to one another and, over time, to develop mutual respect.

Teachers conduct the classes with highly detailed guides for leading the discussions. The leader's role is to be aware of the class dynamics and carefully judge whether and how to intervene to encourage students to refer to the text or to clarify their thinking. Teacher professional development, while helpful and available from the Touchstones Discussion Project, is not required, since the teacher guides are comprehensive. School systems may also rent or purchase a five-hour videotape to assist teachers. Support via the Internet is also available. Some teacher leaders in schools meet regularly to help each other as they develop management skills and share information on their students' progress.

6+1 TRAITS™ of Writing

Northwest Regional Educational Laboratory (NWREL)
101 SW Main Street, Suite 500
Portland, OR 97204
Phone: (503) 275-9500
Website: http:// www.nwrel.org/eval/writing
Grade Levels: K–12

The *6+1 TRAITS* program is based on the premise that once both teachers and students learn the fundamental characteristics of good writing, they can assess and improve their own writing. The six traits of good writing that the program identifies are ideas, organization, voice, word choice, sentence fluency, and conventions. The "+1" trait is presentation: handwriting, formatting, and layout. The program provides instructional strategies and materials to teach students the attributes of each trait and uses student writing and published materials as models of both strong and weak writing. It employs assessment tools, including rubrics (scoring guides) and portfolios, to guide students in revising their written work. *6+1 TRAITS* is designed so that teachers can use it to strengthen their teaching without supplanting their current curriculum materials. Research shows that student writing improves when students receive instruction in the six traits.

With teachers using rubrics and portfolios to evaluate student growth in writing, *6+1 TRAITS* offers a helpful structure and language for teaching and evaluating student writing. Introductory institutes and a "training of trainers" workshop are available. School districts can also arrange for one or two days of on-site professional development for teachers. The book *Creating Writers: Linking Assessment and Writing Instruction* (White Plains, NY: Longman, 1990) by Vicki Spandel and Richard J. Stiggins, two of the originators of the model, also describes six-trait-based instruction and assessment.

> One of a group of middle school teachers who are developing a resource library of picture books to illustrate the traits explained, "I believe the best way to help students understand and recognize the traits in their writing and in other people's writing is to use picture books. We now have about 120 picture books that are used as examples in the trait writing, in the scoring and assessing. In our English department meetings, one teacher will share the trait she is emphasizing right now in the classroom and the picture books she has used. She will bring in her students' writing for the teachers to assess student progress in the trait."

Professional Development Resources

National Writing Project

The National Writing Project (NWP) is a professional development model with the goal of improving writing and learning in the nation's schools. Built upon the model of "teachers teaching teachers," the program begins with invitations to exemplary teachers of all grade levels and disciplines to attend a five-week summer institute that focuses on studying and teaching writing. Teachers who attend the summer institute learn to offer professional development in the form of multiple workshops in their own schools and communities during the school year.

The program began in 1974 as the Bay Area Writing Project at the University of California, Berkeley. It currently has over 11,000 teacher leaders at 150 sites in 48 states. Each NWP site works in partnership with a local university. NWP sites offer a variety of professional development programs tailored to the local needs of teachers and students. A core premise of the program since its inception has been that teachers of writing must be writers and experience what they ask (or should ask) of their own students, which is to write and share drafts with their peers. Teacher leaders are encouraged to continue participating in the editing/response groups they join at the institute. Another essential element of the program involves introducing teachers to the research and literature in the field of writing, thus bridging the gap that often exists between research and practice.

For more information, contact
National Writing Project
University of California, Berkeley
5511 Tolman Hall #1042
Berkeley, CA 94720-1042
Phone: (510) 642-0963
Website: http://www.writingproject.org

> The impact of the National Writing Project on teachers can be profound, as one middle school teacher reported: "The National Writing Project has had the greatest impact on how I shape my classroom and how I address student learning." This teacher stressed the importance of bringing writing and literature into the content areas to help her rural students make personal connections to the content. Noting that her students have markedly increased their scores in state reading and language arts performance assessments since she became involved in the National Writing Project, she said, "I know that professional development is such a key element. It takes a different type of in-depth experience to teach teachers to begin to use literature and writing across the curriculum than it does to just get them to use a journal."

Joellen Killion, *What Works in the Middle: Results-Based Staff Development* (Oxford, Ohio: National Staff Development Council, 1999)

This guide provides information and resources to aid in the selection, design, and evaluation of staff development programs in language arts, mathematics, science, social studies, and interdisciplinary studies. The premise of the guide is that the strong link between teacher learning and student achievement argues for professional development that will help teachers deepen their content area expertise and develop the instructional approaches that allow them to teach content effectively. The book is designed to provide guidance for implementing successful professional development in middle schools. It reviews 26 professional development programs that have demonstrated effects on student learning; seven of these are programs with language arts as a focus.

Available from:
National Staff Development Council
P.O. Box 240
Oxford, OH 45056
Phone: (513) 523-6029
Website: http://www.nsdc.org

Published Literature Programs and Anthologies

The major publishers of language arts materials offer secondary literature series, usually spanning grades 6 through 12. Many of the teachers interviewed for this guide use one or another of the series and find them useful resources, particularly because of the variety of selections they offer and their thematic focus. Several teachers also noted that these volumes save them work in integrating the different aspects of their language arts program. (In some districts, teachers are required to use one of these texts.) Other teachers prefer to select literature and construct their curricula around themes that link more directly to their students' interests and needs.

Selections in these series include historical and contemporary works, works from a variety of cultures, and a range of genres. The volumes in these series also offer suggestions for teaching reading strategies, keeping reading logs or journals, writing and conducting writer's workshops, teaching vocabulary and grammar, and preparing students for assessments. They generally include suggestions for using the Internet and other technology resources. The publishers of these series also offer supplementary materials, including audio versions of the literature selections, videotaped performances of some selections, and various electronic resources. Some materials are available in Spanish as well as English.

Because these series tend to be so similar, this section does not attempt to describe each of them in detail. We offer some highlights and encourage you to contact the publishers, examine the books, and think carefully about whether and how these books can help you and your students meet the goals of your language arts program.

Pegasus

Kendall/Hunt Publishing Company
4050 Westman Drive
P.O. Box 1840
Dubuque, IA 52004-1840
Phone: (800) KH-BOOKS
Website: http://www.kendallhunt.com
Grade Levels: K–6

Pegasus offers a series of theme-based literature units (nine at each grade level), each of which is based upon a complete book. A teacher's guide containing detailed instructional plans and materials accompanies each book. Each unit is intended to be taught over a three- to four-week period. Although *Pegasus* is primarily an elementary program, middle-grades teachers use the sixth-grade book. Its titles include *Dragonwings, Summer of the Monkeys,* and *Number the Stars.* An accompanying hardcover anthology for each grade level includes theme-related short stories, poetry, and nonfiction. A teacher's resource book contains the scope and sequence, daily language activities, a curriculum and skills matrix, and a classroom assessment checklist. A teacher's implementation guide includes strategies for teaching comprehension, writing, and discussion. All of the teacher materials contain numerous models of student work.

Students can read theme-related books listed in each guide's annotated bibliography and self-selected books during independent reading time.

A daily writing workshop ensures that students write on a daily basis and that writing assignments are related to the literature. *Pegasus* also makes connections across the curriculum, with an emphasis on literature, science, health, geography, social science/current events, and history. The program can be taught in 60-minute periods, but the implementation guide also offers suggestions about how to integrate it with other content areas in longer blocks of time.

A sixth-grade teacher who has used *Pegasus* for five years explained why her school chose this program: "It links directly to our state curriculum. It uses rich literature instead of only parts of a story. It has a tight scope and sequence that provides continuity across the grades. It gives you the structure, yet it allows for freedom as well. And it was written by teachers. The program has books and topics about which you can feel passionate. It also links to other things that we have to teach. Many of the novels have a direct correlation to social studies and to science. So it allows you to teach smarter not harder. Students are talking about the literature—the characters, opinions, issues—in groups, they're writing about it, and simultaneously they're preparing for the state writing test."

Glencoe Literature Program

Glencoe/McGraw-Hill
Customer Service Department
P.O. Box 544
Blacklick, OH 43004-0544
Phone: (800) 334-7344
Website: http://lit.glencoe.com
Grade Levels: 6–12

Each grade-level volume is organized around a series of themes. For seventh grade, for example, themes include "What I Am, What I Want to Be," "Winds of Change," "Facing Challenge," and "Where the Heart Is." Selections include short stories, nonfiction, poetry, drama, myths, legends, folktales, songs, comic strips, scripts, and advertisements. Particular genres are highlighted at each level, and the books also feature "Media Connections" (e.g., newspaper and magazine articles, websites, comics), comparisons of some reading selections, active reading strategies tied to particular genres, interdisciplinary connections, and guidelines for writing workshops on particular genres. Skills instruction addresses grammar; listening, speaking, and viewing; reading and thinking skills; technology skills; vocabulary; and writing skills. The books also offer a variety of assessment resources, including "selection quick checks" to assess comprehension; comprehensive tests for each selection and theme; performance assessment tasks with accompanying rubrics; student models and assessment rubrics for each writing workshop activity; forms, checklists, and tips for managing portfolios; and standardized test practice at the end of each theme.

Teacher resources include planning guides and information about block scheduling, inclusion strategies, and literature groups; transparencies; a variety of skills lessons and activities; assessment materials; a sourcebook for English language learners; and a collection of Spanish resources. An audio library is also available in Spanish as well as English.

Elements of Literature
Holt, Rinehart and Winston
1120 S. Capital of Texas Highway
Austin, TX 78746-6487
Phone: (512) 314-6500
Website: http://www.hrw.com
Grade Levels: 6–12

Grades 6, 7, and 8 in this series are organized into thematic "Collections" and include a variety of genres and a mix of historical and contemporary works. Themes for grade 7 include, for example, "Out Here On My Own: Facing Challenges," "Who Am I?: A Rose By Any Other Name Might Be a Daisy," "Do the Right Thing: Making Difficult Choices," and "We Rookies Have to Stick Together: Buddies Forever." Features include a "Before You Read" section to prepare and motivate students to read the selections, "Meet the Writer" sections, and related selections (including magazine articles, letters, and poems) that link to the ideas and themes in the main selections. Among the additional features are reading skills and strategies, "Quickwrite" prereading exercises, questions to encourage personal and critical response, cross-curricular activities, and "Reading for Life" and "Learning for Life" sections intended to help students build practical reading, communication, and thinking skills. Also included are guidelines for the writing process, writing portfolios, writing workshops, and language skills practice (vocabulary, grammar, mechanics, and usage). Assessment resources include tests on individual selections, tests on literary elements, a portfolio management system with rubrics for writing assignments, and standardized test practice.

The program offers an audio CD library with nearly all reading selections; videos with author biographies and interviews, historical information, and other resources (with English and Spanish soundtracks); and language workshop and writer's workshop interactive multimedia CD-ROMs. Teacher resources include planning software, lesson plans with strategies for English language learners, guidelines for managing portfolios and other assessments, and transparencies.

The Language of Literature
McDougal Littell
Customer Service Center
1900 S. Batavia
Geneva, IL 60134
Phone: (800) 323-5435
Website: http://www.mcdougallittell.com
Grade Levels: 6–12

This series includes a variety of literature selections intended to be of interest to middle-grades students and to represent a variety of cultures. Each book is organized into a series of thematic units. In the grade 7 volume, for example, themes include "Learning from Experience," "Relationships," "Flights of Imagination," and "Nothing Stays the Same." Genres include short stories, poetry, narrative nonfiction, essays, autobiography, memoir, biography, drama, magazine and newspaper articles, Internet articles, fables, folktales, myths, oral parables, oral history, interviews, songs, and instructions. Each unit is in two parts, and each part focuses on active reading strategies for a particular genre. "Literary Links" provides additional, related literary selections; "Real World Links" provides magazine articles or other theme-related nonfiction selections as well as relevant research skills. Additional features include connections to other curriculum areas, vocabulary and grammar skills, guidelines for writing workshops on particular genres, author studies, suggested readings at the end of each unit for extending learning, and cross-cultural connections. Assessment resources include tests on individual selections, standardized test practice, writing prompts with scoring rubrics, guidelines for portfolio assessment, and other suggestions for integrating assessment into literacy activities.

The program offers an audio library, videotaped versions of some selections, and a variety of other electronic resources (CD-ROM, videodisc, website). Teacher resources also include an organizational guide for each grade level, unit resource books, lesson plans, a sourcebook for English language learners, a Spanish study guide, a guide to assessment, and transparencies.

Prentice Hall Literature
Prentice Hall
4350 Equity Drive
P.O. Box 2649
Columbus, OH 43216-2649
Phone: (800) 848-9500
Website: http://www.phschool.com
Grade Levels: 7–12
Each grade level volume in this series (Grade 6, Copper; Grade 7, Bronze; Grade 8, Silver) organizes its selections by genre: short story, drama, nonfiction (e.g., biography, letters, essays, articles from the media), poetry, the oral or folk tradition (e.g., fables, folktales, trickster tales, myths), and the novel (including a complete novel). Each selection begins with a "Guide to Reading" which includes background information, an author biography, a literary concept to focus on, and a vocabulary list. Most selections also conclude with a "Reading and Responding" section which focuses on literary elements of the text. Also included are reading strategies intended to foster comprehension and critical response to the selections. Other sections encompass the writing process, specific reading skills (e.g., making inferences, comparing and contrasting), and extension activities designed to integrate the language arts. Each volume

includes three brief handbooks: one each on the writing process, grammar and revising strategies, and literary terms and techniques. Assessment resources include a variety of tests on selections and entire units, including comprehension items, essay questions, and reader response questions; guidelines for evaluating student writing; models of strong and weak student writing, and standardized test preparation materials.

The program also offers multimedia resources, including CD-ROMs, audiocassettes of the student book, "Interest Grabber" and other video-tapes, English and Spanish summaries, and Spanish readings on audio CD. Teacher resources include an assessment guide, reading process guide, and guide to speaking, listening, viewing, and representing; class-room tips from "master teachers"; art, music, and humanities connections; transparencies; a variety of skills lessons and activities; assessment materials; and additional Spanish support resources.

Student Reference

Write Source 2000: A Guide to Writing, Thinking and Learning

Great Source Education Group, Houghton Mifflin
P.O. Box 7050
Wilmington, MA 01887
Phone: (800) 289-4490
Website: www.greatsource.com
Grade Levels: 6–8

Write Source 2000 is a resource handbook that stresses the fundamental principles of writing. It covers the writing process, forms of writing, and writing mechanics, and also includes research tips. Visually appealing to middle-grades students, the handbook includes many models of student writing and is a useful reference and guide. Several of the teachers interviewed for this guide recommended *Write Source 2000*. Great Source also offers the *Write Source 2000 Language Program* which includes a program guide in a binder with daily lesson plans for teachers and a student skills book.

Management Tools

Accelerated Reader

Renaissance Learning
P.O. Box 8036
Wisconsin Rapids, WI 54495
Phone: (888) 656-2931
Website: http://renlearn.com
Grade Level: PreK–12

Accelerated Reader is a computerized learning information system that assesses students' reading comprehension of selected books and tracks student performance via multiple-choice quizzes that students take after reading a book. Described as a technology-based literacy program, it aims to promote reading and thereby improve student achievement. Renaissance Learning has developed computerized quizzes for over 19,000 books, all of them rated by reading level. The software creates individualized student progress reports. Also available is the STAR reading test and database, which allows for a quick assessment of students' reading level. STAR identifies the range of difficulty in which a student is challenged yet able to succeed without frustration.

Renaissance Learning offers different packages to schools, ranging from basic starter kits to more comprehensive kits, depending on the number of quizzes purchased and the amount of technical support provided. Books are purchased separately. The company also offers seminars to help teachers learn to use the program.

More than 40 percent of schools in Texas use *Accelerated Reader*. Among the teachers we interviewed for this guide, several Texas teachers who use the program reported that their students were reading more, especially since they allotted class time for using the program. One teacher, whose school required the use of *Accelerated Reader* for at least one six-week block during the school year, observed that "one of the best things for the kids is they read a book, they take a test, and because they are reading on their own level, they're successful. That builds their confidence and desire to read more. This is just one piece of our language arts program and it's no substitute for a challenging, integrated curriculum. But it is effective in what it does."

Scholastic Reading Counts!™ Software System
Scholastic, Inc.
2931 East McCarty Street
Jefferson City, MO 65101
Phone: (800) 724-6527
(877) 268-6871 (for a catalog)
Website: http://www.scholastic.com
Grade Levels: K–12

This software product provides a database of books at a range of reading levels along with quizzes based on the books. For each grade level, *Scholastic Reading Counts!* offers collections of quizzes on books that are related by theme, genre, topic, reading level, author, or other category. Each collection contains quizzes for 30 titles. The software also allows teachers to create their own quiz collections (from a database of 15,000 titles) and provides management tools for selecting reading material, monitoring student progress in various reporting formats, and customizing the program. Students can also monitor their own progress. Scholastic offers a variety of packages, ranging from a starter pack to more comprehensive collections, differing in the number of quiz collections and amount of technical support provided. Books are purchased separately. Beginning in the fall of 2000, Scholastic is offering professional development seminars for teachers, school librarians, media specialists, and others interested in building independent reading programs.

Professional Materials

Many of the teachers interviewed for this guide mentioned that one or more of the books listed in this section had strongly influenced their thinking and practice. These books provide both theoretical and practical guidance for literacy educators, drawing on a growing research base about how middle-grades students become thoughtful and engaged readers, effective communicators, and analytic and critical thinkers.

A number of the resources described in this section are available from four publishers: The Association for Supervision and Curriculum Development (ASCD), Heinemann (or Heinemann-Boynton/Cook), the National Council of Teachers of English (NCTE), and Stenhouse. Contact information for these four is provided at the end of this section; contact information for other resources is listed with the individual resources. Books are listed alphabetically by author.

Allen, Janet, *It's Never Too Late: Leading Adolescents to Lifelong Literacy* (Portsmouth, NH: Heinemann, 1995)

Allen describes her own experiences teaching "at-risk" adolescents and uses case studies to describe strategies for teaching reading and writing to struggling middle and high school students. She addresses such challenges as building a classroom environment to support strategic learning, being creative in finding resources when funding is scarce, and dealing with resistant and disruptive students. The book's appendices include examples of assessment prompts and other tools Allen has developed.

Allen, Janet, and Kyle Gonzalez, *There's Room for Me Here: Literacy Workshop in the Middle School* (York, ME: Stenhouse, 1998)

Allen and Gonzalez describe in detail a literacy workshop approach that incorporates a wide variety of strategies designed to individualize instruction. They focus on the experience of new teacher Gonzalez's Florida middle school students who struggle with reading and writing. The book includes detailed information about classroom layout and daily schedules; using "read-alouds" and shared, guided, and independent reading; creating a balanced writing program; and helping students set goals and evaluate their own progress. The authors provide photographs, examples of students' work, record-keeping forms, samples of graphic organizers, and lists of suggested books for independent and shared reading.

Applebee, Arthur N., *Curriculum as Conversation: Transforming Traditions of Teaching and Learning* **(Chicago: University of Chicago Press, 1996)**

Applebee contrasts the traditional view of curriculum in which students are taught the accumulated knowledge of the past with a view of curriculum as giving students the tools to participate in ongoing conversations about important ideas. The challenge for curriculum development is to create contexts for students to engage in conversations within the domains of discourse that characterize various disciplines, and the challenge for instruction is to help students learn to participate in these conversations. Throughout the book, Applebee both locates his argument within historical trends in curriculum and provides concrete examples of how teachers can transform the secondary English curriculum into a vital conversation.

Available from:
The University of Chicago Press
5801 South Ellis
Chicago, IL 60637
(773) 702-7700
http://www.press.uchicago.edu

Atwell, Nancie, *In the Middle: New Understandings About Writing, Reading, and Learning,* **Second Edition (Portsmouth, NH: Heinemann-Boynton/Cook, 1998)**

This volume is a significantly revised and expanded version of Atwell's influential 1987 book which introduced the literacy workshop approach to middle-grades language arts teachers. In the new edition, Atwell continues to urge teachers to create curriculum with their students, but she also offers ways for teachers to intervene more directly to establish procedures for writing workshops, teach conventions, analyze and respond to literature, and introduce different genres. The book includes lists of mini-lessons with examples of how Atwell teaches them, guidelines for record keeping, and forms for tracking individual students' spelling, skills, homework, writing, and reading.

Beane, James (Ed.), *Toward a Coherent Curriculum: 1995 Yearbook of the Association for Supervision and Curriculum Development* **(Alexandria, VA: Association for Supervision and Curriculum Development, 1995)**

This volume focuses on ways that educators are trying to make the curriculum, both within and across subject areas, more coherent. In his introduction, Beane contends that for students, trying to make sense of the disconnected information and skills that constitute the school curriculum can be as frustrating and pointless as trying to put together a jigsaw puzzle without having the whole picture in front of you. He defines a coherent curriculum as one "that makes sense as a whole; and its parts, whatever they are, are unified and connected by that sense of the whole." Achieving such coherence, he argues, requires connections not only among the various components of students' experiences in school, but also connections between those experiences and students' lives outside of school. "When the curriculum offers a sense of purpose, unity, relevance, and pertinence . . . young people are more likely to integrate educational experiences into their schemes of meaning, which in turn broadens and deepens their understanding of themselves and the world." The book is divided into three sections. The first raises questions about and suggests some possible features of a coherent curriculum. The second section describes a number of approaches to creating coherence, drawing on both theory and examples of practice, and considers coherence within, across, and beyond the disciplines. This section addresses such issues as curriculum organization, use of themes, and assessment. The third section offers commentaries on the approaches described in the previous section.

Calkins, Lucy McCormick, *The Art of Teaching Writing*, New Edition (Portsmouth, NH: Heinemann, 1994)

The first edition of this book, published in 1986, introduced many teachers to the writing workshop and the idea that the best writing is on topics students initiate and care about. In the new edition, Calkins describes how her ideas about teaching writing have developed in the interim, responds to questions that teachers have asked her about how to make writing workshops work in their classrooms, and, in a chapter on creating mini-lessons, advises teachers not to be "afraid to teach." Calkins traces how writing develops starting in the early grades, but includes a chapter on "Teaching Adolescents." The new edition also contains chapters on assessment, thematic studies, nonfiction writing, and home-school connections.

Daniels, Harvey, *Literature Circles: Voice and Choice in the Student-Centered Classroom* (York, ME: Stenhouse, 1994)

Daniels focuses on ways to make student-led discussion groups work in the classroom. Literature circles offer a means for teachers to encourage independent reading, drawing on methods used in collaborative learning, including assigning students responsibility for particular roles. Based on the experiences of 22 teachers from kindergarten through college, Daniels offers practical guidance on getting literature circles started and managing them over time.

Delpit, Lisa D., *Other People's Children: Cultural Conflict in the Classroom* (New York: The New Press, 1995)

This book collects nine of Delpit's essays and book chapters on various aspects of cultural diversity in education. Delpit argues that many of the academic problems encountered by children of color result from miscommunication as schools steeped in the dominant culture struggle with the inequality and imbalance of power in our society. Two of the pieces included in the book are "Skills and Other Dilemmas of a Black Educator" and "The Silenced Dialogue," which prompted a great deal of debate among literacy educators when they were originally published in the late 1980s. In these papers, Delpit offers a critique of writing process pedagogy and voices minority educators' concerns that their voices are not heard in the dialogue about literacy instruction. She contends that, while all students benefit from writing for real purposes and audiences, students who do not come to school experienced in the language of the dominant culture benefit from explicit instruction in its conventions.

Available from:
The New Press
450 West 41st Street, 6th Floor
New York, NY 10036
(800) 233-4830
http:// www.thenewpress.com

Graves, Donald H., *A Fresh Look at Writing* (Portsmouth, NH: Heinemann, 1994) and *Bring Life into Learning: Create a Lasting Literacy* (Portsmouth, NH: Heinemann, 1999)

Graves's pathbreaking 1983 book *Writing: Teachers and Children at Work* introduced many teachers to the concept of the writing process and influenced many of the other authors whose works are included in this list of resources. In *A Fresh Look at Writing,* Graves expands his ideas for creating lifelong writers and learners. He considers portfolios, record keeping, the teaching of conventions, spelling, and writing in a variety of genres. In the more recent work *Bring Life into Learning,* Graves argues that the human aspect of various disciplines should become the focus of learning. Each chapter suggests "Actions" that illustrate how teachers can do this as they teach essential knowledge and skills in social studies, science, and the arts.

Keene, Ellin Oliver, and Susan Zimmermann, *Mosaic of Thought: Teaching Comprehension in a Reader's Workshop* (Portsmouth, NH: Heinemann, 1997)

Keene and Zimmermann consider how teachers can help students who struggle with reading to learn the strategies proficient readers use and thereby become more independent, flexible, and motivated readers. The authors advocate explicit instruction in these strategies within a literature-rich classroom. Strategies they advocate include connecting with students' existing knowledge, focusing on sensory images, asking questions, drawing inferences, and identifying what's important. The book draws on the authors' and other teachers' experience as both readers and teachers.

Langer, Judith, *Beating the Odds: Teaching Middle and High School Students to Read and Write Well* (Albany: Center for English Learning and Achievement, State University of New York at Albany, 1999)

Langer reports on the first three years of a five-year study designed to identify features of English instruction that distinguish secondary schools in which students are performing at higher levels than comparable schools on statewide "high-stakes" tests. She identifies six characteristics of the language arts programs in these "beat the odds" schools which work together to increase students' achievement: (1) balanced use of direct instruction of isolated skills, "simulated" instruction in which students apply concepts and skills in structured exercises, and "integrated" instruction in which students use skills and knowledge in the context of a "large and purposeful activity"; (2) integration of test preparation into ongoing learning; (3) explicit connections of knowledge, skills, and ideas across lessons, classes, and grades, as well as between in-school and out-of-school applications; (4) teaching students strategies for thinking about (planning, organizing, or reflecting on content or an activity) as well as carrying out activities; (5) moving beyond achievement of immediate learning goals to deeper understanding and student-generated ideas; (6) treatment of literacy learning as a social activity, with groups of students engaged in substantive discussion of ideas from multiple perspectives. Langer notes that these six features work together to help students achieve what she calls "higher literacy": "the ability to use language, content, and reasoning in ways that are appropriate for particular situations and disciplines."

Available from:
Center on English Learning & Achievement
School of Education
State University of New York at Albany
1400 Washington Avenue
Albany, NY 12222
(518) 442-5026
http://cela.albany.edu

National Council of Teachers of English, *Teaching Literature in Middle School: Fiction* and *Motivating Writing in Middle School* (Urbana, IL: National Council of Teachers of English, 1996)

These two volumes, both part of NCTE's *Standards Consensus Series,* are collections of brief teaching ideas designed to provide language arts teachers with suggestions for aligning their teaching practices with local, state, and national standards. These volumes contain useful and creative suggestions, ranging from using dialogue journals and mini-lessons to teach about literary elements to engaging students in recommending multicultural literature to their peers; from activities to encourage writing fluency to teaching specific revision strategies. These ideas serve as illustrations of particular practices rather than as a blueprint for constructing a coherent curriculum.

Rief, Linda, *Seeking Diversity: Language Arts with Adolescents* (Portsmouth, NH: Heinemann, 1992)

Rief traces an academic year in her eighth-grade New Hampshire classroom, showing how she and her students read, write, think, question, and explore experiences and ideas. Rief includes many practical suggestions and samples of students' work at various stages. She talks about organizing the classroom, using life experiences and literature to engage students in meaningful writing and reading, assessment methods that focus on process as well as product and encourage self-evaluation, assembling portfolios, and integrating art into literacy learning. Appendices include a booklist and sample handouts for students and parents.

Rief, Linda, *Vision and Voice: Extending the Literacy Spectrum* (Portsmouth, NH: Heinemann, 1998)

This volume extends the ideas about using the arts in teaching literacy that Rief introduced in her earlier volume, encouraging teachers to expand their ideas of literacy to include the visual and oral arts. The book focuses on two large-scale student research projects, one on the environment of the rain forest and the other on the textile mills of the Industrial Revolution. In addition to a number of brief vignettes that provide practical suggestions for including the visual and oral arts in the language arts classroom, the book includes a companion CD-ROM with color photographs and the voices of students.

Short, Kathy G., and Carolyn Burke, *Creating Curriculum: Teachers and Students as a Community of Learners* (Portsmouth, NH: Heinemann, 1991)

In this brief (72-page) volume, Short and Burke encourage teachers to rethink curriculum not as the content prescribed by textbooks, as district scope and sequence, or as a collection of unconnected activities, but as a shared process that teachers and students negotiate, developing and implementing the curriculum collaboratively. This notion of curriculum focuses on inquiry and the search for questions that matter to learners, and on ongoing reflection about the learning process as well as its content. The authors do not contend that input from curriculum developers, administrators, and other experts outside the classroom should be ignored, but that both teachers and students should examine it thoughtfully and critically.

Tchudi, Stephen, *Planning and Assessing the Curriculum in English Language Arts* (Alexandria, VA: Association for Supervision and Curriculum Development, 1991)

Tchudi focuses on the philosophical and practical issues in English language arts curriculum development. The book is in three parts: Part One provides a historical overview of the evolution of language arts programs and notes the promising features of recent trends in the field. Part Two traces the development of examples of successful programs. Part Three offers guidelines for curriculum development.

Tchudi, Stephen N., and Susan J. Tchudi, *The English/Language Arts Handbook: Classroom Strategies for Teachers* (Portsmouth, NH: Heinemann-Boynton/Cook, 1991)

The authors argue that the most important change in English teaching over the past several decades has been a shift from an "atheoretical" collection of content and instructional practices to a "deepening body of knowledge accurately describing how people go about mastering language."

The book offers both a theory of language and language learning and practical examples of how to apply that theory in the classroom. The first part of the book focuses on planning and setting goals, and the next three parts offer ideas for teaching literature and reading, oral and written composition, and language. The final chapter discusses teaching as a profession.

Wheelock, Anne, *Safe to be Smart: Building a Culture for Standards-Based Reform in the Middle Grades* (Columbus, OH: National Middle School Association, 1998)

Wheelock argues that in order to achieve high standards schools must change the way they operate as well as the content of their curricula. Schools committed to standards-based reforms create cultures that support the beliefs that (1) every student can think well and understand deeply (i.e., "become smart"), and (2) the school and its teachers are responsible for enabling students to learn in a way that develops deep understanding. Wheelock draws from many schools and classrooms to illustrate the kinds of practices that follow from these beliefs. These practices include making expectations clear and explicit to students; a focus on student work, supported by good teaching and challenging curriculum; building relationships with students that foster motivation, effort, and investment in schoolwork; and development of professional communities of teachers that focus on achieving high expectations for all students.

Available from:
National Middle School Association
4151 Executive Parkway, Suite 300
Westerville, OH 43081
(800) 528-6672
http://www.nmsa.org

Wilhelm, Jeffrey D., *Standards in Practice, Grades 6–8 Series* (Urbana, IL: National Council of Teachers of English, 1996)

A companion to the *Standards for the English Language Arts* developed by NCTE and IRA, this book is a narrative account of how the teachers and students in one middle school worked together to craft a curriculum that uses the standards as the basis for literacy learning. The book highlights strategies that students use to reflect on their own learning, as well as their use of hypermedia to design their own learning activities. Included are samples of teacher handouts and student work, as well as lists of resources. Wilhelm also identifies particular standards addressed by various components of the curriculum.

Wilhelm, Jeffrey D., *"You Gotta BE the Book": Teaching Engaged and Reflective Reading with Adolescents* (New York: Teachers College Press, 1997)

Using three case studies of seventh-grade readers drawn from his own teaching experience, Wilhelm shows how use of drama and art can enable previously unsuccessful and unmotivated middle-grades students to become eager and passionate readers. Wilhelm considers what is rewarding and engaging about reading to students who love to read, and why other students come to hate it. He draws on the work of literary theorists and reading researchers to contrast a view of reading as receiving meaning with a view of reading as creating meaning, and he describes how to enact the latter view in the classroom. The book includes an appendix that suggests questions and activities for what Wilhelm calls the "Ten Dimensions of Reader Response": entering the story world, showing interest in the story action, relating to characters, seeing the story world, elaborating on the story world, connecting literature to life, considering significance, recognizing literary conventions, recognizing reading as a transaction, and evaluating an author and the self as reader.

Available from NCTE and from:
Teachers College Press
P.O. Box 20
Williston, VT 05495-0020
(800) 575-6566
http://www.teacherscollegepress.com

Association for Supervision and Curriculum Development (ASCD)
1703 North Beauregard Street
Alexandria, VA 22311-1714
(703) 578-9600
http://www.ascd.org

Heinemann (and Heinemann-Boynton/Cook)
88 Post Road
P.O. Box 5007
Westport, CT 06881
(800) 793-2154
http://www.heinemann.com

National Council of Teachers of English (NCTE)
1111 W. Kenyon Road
Urbana, IL 61801-1096
800-369-6283
http://www.ncte.org

Stenhouse Publishers
P.O. Box 1929
Columbus, OH 43216-1929
(800) 988-9812
FAX (614) 487-2272
http://www.stenhouse.com

Publisher Contact Information